GLUTEN-FREE BR

MACHINE COOKBOOK

The Comprehensive Step-by-Step Guide To Making Delicious Bread Recipes With Your Bread Machine

Meng Hsüeh

Table Of Contents

INTRODUCTION

Once upon a time, a kitchen filled with laughter, warmth, and an irresistible aroma that seemed to linger in the air—a fragrance from freshly baked bread's alchemy. In this kitchen, the heart of every meal was woven from flour, water, and a dash of magic.

Yet, amid this culinary symphony, there was a quest—a quest for those seeking the perfect slice of bread, one that wasn't just delicious but also free from the constraints of gluten. It was a noble pursuit, a journey through trials and triumphs, an odyssey that sparked the creation of this very cookbook.

Picture this: a family, eager to share meals, faced with the challenge of gluten intolerance. The aroma of bread baking in the oven was a long-lost memory, replaced by the uncertainty of store-bought loaves that often lacked the heartwarming taste and texture they craved.

Enter the hero of our tale: the trusty bread machine. With ingenuity, experimentation, and a touch of perseverance, this kitchen champion became the gateway to a world of gluten-free delight. From humble beginnings to triumphs in the kitchen, the quest for the perfect gluten-free loaf was finally within reach.

And now, dear reader, you hold in your hands the culmination of this adventure—a treasury of recipes meticulously crafted and tested, each one a testament to the joy of gluten-free baking with the beloved bread machine. From the whispers of white bread to the robust melodies of artisanal creations, every page of this cookbook is an invitation to join this flavorful journey.

Here, within these pages, you'll find not just recipes but a roadmap through the world of gluten-free baking. With insights into ingredients, tips for troubleshooting, and a bounty of diverse recipes, this cookbook aims to empower you on your quest for the perfect gluten-free bread, all with the convenience and magic of your faithful bread machine.

So, embark on this adventure. Let the aroma of freshly baked bread fill your kitchen once more. Let the joy of creating and savoring each slice be your guide. Welcome to the gluten-free bread revolution—where every recipe tells a story, and each bite is a triumph of flavor and nourishment.

CHAPTER 1

Alternatives and Substitutes

Substitutes for flour:

Rice flour is a versatile option that comes in white or brown varieties. It has a mild flavor and a lighter texture.

Almond flour adds richness and moisture to baked goods but cannot be used as a one-to-one replacement due to its higher fat content.

Coconut Flour: Because it is highly absorbent, it requires more liquid. It has a distinct flavor profile and a dense texture.

Quinoa Flour: Provides a nutty flavor as well as a protein boost. Because of its slightly gritty texture, it works well in blends.

Buckwheat Flour: Despite its name, this gluten-free flour adds a robust, earthy flavor. Best when combined with other flours.

Agents of Binding:

Xanthan Gum: This substance mimics the binding properties of gluten. Use sparingly because too much can cause a gummy texture.

Guar Gum is another xanthan gum substitute. It's made from guar beans and acts as a thickener and binding agent.

Substitutes for Liquids:

Dairy Substitutes: Lactose-free alternatives include almond, soy, oat, or coconut milk.

Water or broth: For a different flavor profile, replace certain fruit juices or alcoholic beverages in recipes with water or broth.

Agents of leavening:

Baking powder: Check the label to make sure it's gluten-free, as some brands may contain gluten derivatives.

Yeast is naturally gluten-free, but it must be fresh and within its expiration date to perform optimally.

Egg substitutes:

Chia or flax eggs: To make a gel-like substitute for eggs, combine ground flaxseeds or chia seeds with water.

Commercial Egg Substitutes: These powdered substitutes, which are available in stores, work well in a variety of recipes.

Herbs and spices: Boost flavor profiles and add depth to gluten-free bread. Experiment with cinnamon, rosemary, garlic, and other ingredients.

Nuts and seeds add texture and nutritional value. To add variety, mix in sunflower seeds, pumpkin seeds, almonds, or walnuts.

Suggestions for Substitutions:

Flours to Blend: Experiment with various flour blends to improve texture and flavor.

Ratios to Follow: To avoid dry or dense results understand the wet-to-dry ingredient ratios when using alternative flours.

Adjust Liquid Content: Because some flours absorb more liquid than others, the liquid content should be adjusted accordingly.

Binding Agents should be combined: To improve structure, combine xanthan or guar gum with other binding agents.

What to do if your bread machine lacks gluten-free settings

What gluten-free bread machine setting do you use?

If your bread machine does not have a gluten-free setting, choose the one with the fewest mixing cycles (often the quick, rapid, rapid rise, one rise, or basic feature). You can also override the preset settings for a 20-minute mix cycle, a 1-hour rise cycle, and a 1-hour bake cycle.

CHAPTER 2

GLUTEN-FREE BREAD RECIPES

Cinnamon Raisin Gluten-Free Bread

Ingredients

Wet Ingredients

- *3 eggs*
- *1 cup water*
- *½ cup almond milk*
- *3 Tablespoons vegetable oil*
- *1 teaspoon cider vinegar*
- *2 Tablespoons Honey*
- *2 ¼ teaspoons instant yeast*
- *340 grams of white rice flour*
- *100 grams of potato starch*
- *40 grams of tapioca flour*
- *¼ cup flaxseed meal*
- *3 teaspoons psyllium husk*
- *1 ½ teaspoons salt*
- *3 Tbsp. Swerve sugar replacer or white sugar*
- *3 teaspoons cinnamon*
- *½ cup raisins*

Instructions

1. All ingredients should be at room temperature, 70 – 80 F.
2. In a medium bowl, combine the dry ingredients. Mix thoroughly and set aside.
3. In a medium bowl, combine the wet ingredients. Whisk thoroughly and set aside.
4. Add the wet ingredients to the bread machine pan. Then pour the dry ingredients on top.
5. Make a shallow well in the center and add the yeast.

6. Select the gluten-free cycle setting on your bread maker. Then select the 2-pound loaf.

7. Around 3 minutes into mixing, open the lid and use a spatula to clear the sides of the pan, avoiding the paddle. Check and scrape edges and under the dough during kneading. Adjust dough consistency with small amounts of flour blend or warm water if needed. Keep the lid closed during rise and bake cycles.

8. After baking, check the bread temperature (97°C to 99°C) with a thermometer. Remove the pan and place it on a wire rack. Let it sit for a few minutes, then turn the pan upside down to release the loaf. If needed, carefully remove the paddle from the bottom. Allow the bread to cool upside down for at least 2 hours before slicing.

Traditional Egg Bread

Ingredients

- *2 teaspoons instant yeast*
- *2 1/4 cups Light Flour Blend*
- *1 1/4 cups millet flour*
- *1/4 cup milk powder*
- *2 tablespoons granulated cane sugar*
- *2 1/2 teaspoons baking powder*
- *1 teaspoon xanthan gum*
- *1/2 teaspoon kosher or fine sea salt*
- *1/8 teaspoon ascorbic acid (optional)*
- *1 tablespoon honey or agave nectar*
- *3/4 cup warmed water (27°C)*
- *3 large eggs, beaten*
- *6 tablespoons melted salted butter, slightly cooled*
- *2 teaspoons apple cider vinegar*

Instructions:

1. All ingredients should be at room temperature, 70 – 80 F.

2. Set up the bread pan and beater paddle(s). Add wet ingredients first, followed by dry ingredients into the pan.

3. Combine yeast in a small bowl. Mix the remaining dry ingredients in a large bowl thoroughly.

4. Whisk honey and water in a glass measuring cup. Add other wet ingredients, whisk again, and pour into the bread pan. Spread dry ingredients evenly over the liquids, creating a well in the center for the yeast.

5. Set the bread pan in the machine, secure it, and choose settings: Gluten-free cycle, 1 1/2 pounds loaf, medium crust, then start.

6. Around 3 minutes into mixing, open the lid and use a spatula to clear the sides of the pan, avoiding the paddle. Check and scrape edges and under the dough during kneading. Adjust dough consistency with small amounts of flour blend or warm water if needed. Keep the lid closed during rise and bake cycles.

7. After baking, check the bread temperature (97°C to 99°C) with a thermometer. Remove the pan and place it on a wire rack. Let it sit for a few minutes, then turn the pan upside down to release the loaf. If needed, carefully remove the paddle from the bottom. Allow the bread to cool upside down for at least 2 hours before slicing.

Potato Bread Magic

Ingredients

- *1 tablespoon instant yeast*
- *2 1/2 cups Whole-Grain Flour*
- *1/2 cup potato starch*
- *1/2 cup milk powder*
- *2 tablespoons sugar*
- *2 teaspoons tapioca flour/starch*
- *2 teaspoons psyllium husk flakes or powder*
- *2 teaspoons kosher or fine sea salt*
- *1/8 teaspoon ascorbic acid (optional)*
- *1 1/4 cups warm water (300 ml), about 80°F (27°C)*
- *2 large eggs, beaten*
- *2 teaspoons apple cider vinegar*
- *2 tablespoons melted nondairy butter substitute*
- *1 1/2 cups riced or mashed cooked and peeled potatoes*

Instructions

1. All ingredients should be at room temperature, 70 – 80 F.
2. Set up the bread pan and beater paddle(s). Add wet ingredients first, followed by dry ingredients into the pan.
3. Put yeast in a small bowl aside. Whisk the rest of the dry ingredients in a large mixing bowl.
4. Whisk water, eggs, vinegar, and butter in a glass measuring cup until smooth. Pour into the bread pan. Add potatoes. Spread dry ingredients over wet ones using a spatula, creating a well in the center for the yeast.
5. Set the bread pan in the machine, securing it in place. Choose settings: Gluten-free cycle, 1 1/2 pounds loaf, medium crust, then start.
6. After the initial kneading cycle, use a spatula to ensure all dry ingredients are fully mixed in.
7. Once baked, check the bread's temperature (97°C to 99°C) with a thermometer. Remove the pan and place it on a wire rack. After a few minutes, flip the pan to release the loaf. If needed, carefully remove the paddle from the bottom. Allow the bread to cool upside down for at least 2 hours before slicing.
8. To store, keep the bread in a resealable bag or airtight container at room temperature for up to 3 days. For longer storage, slice and tightly double-wrap each piece before freezing in a resealable plastic bag for up to 3 months.

Flavorful Herb Bread

Ingredients

- *2 tablespoons instant yeast*
- *3 cups Light Flour*
- *1/4 cup granulated cane sugar*
- *1 tablespoon baking powder*
- *2 teaspoons xanthan gum*
- *2 teaspoons kosher salt*
- *1 teaspoon each dried dill weed, oregano, basil, thyme*
- *1 teaspoon onion powder*
- *1/8 teaspoon ascorbic acid (optional)*

- *3 large eggs, beaten*
- *1 cup + 2 tablespoons 1% milk or warm water*
- *1/4 cup olive oil*
- *2 teaspoons apple cider vinegar*

Instructions:

1. All ingredients should be at room temperature, 70 – 80 F.
2. Set up the bread pan and beater paddle(s). Add wet ingredients first, followed by dry ingredients into the pan.
3. Place yeast in a small bowl aside. Whisk the rest of the dry ingredients together in a large mixing bowl.
4. Whisk the wet ingredients in a glass measuring cup and pour into the bread pan. Spread dry ingredients over the wet mixture, ensuring coverage. Create a small well in the center and add the yeast.
5. Set the bread pan into the machine, ensuring it's secure. Choose settings: Gluten-free cycle, 1 1/2 pounds loaf, medium crust, then start.
6. Around 3 minutes after the machine begins mixing, open the lid and use a spatula to clear the pan's sides, avoiding the paddle. Check and scrape any loose flour into the dough during the kneading cycle. Adjust consistency with small amounts of flour blend or warm water if needed. Keep the lid closed during rise and bake cycles.
7. Once baked, check the bread's temperature (97°C to 99°C) using a thermometer. Remove the pan and place it on a wire rack. After a few minutes, flip the pan to release the loaf. If needed, carefully remove the paddle from the bottom. Allow the bread to cool upside down for at least 2 hours before slicing.
8. Store the bread in a resealable bag or airtight container at room temperature for up to 3 days. For longer storage, slice and tightly double-wrap each piece before freezing in a resealable plastic bag for up to 3 months.

Effortless Sorghum Sandwich Bread

Ingredients

- *2 teaspoons instant yeast*

- *2 cups Light Flour Blend*
- *1 cup sorghum flour*
- *1/4 cup granulated cane sugar*
- *1/4 cup milk powder*
- *2 teaspoons xanthan gum*
- *2 teaspoons baking powder*
- *1 teaspoon kosher salt*
- *1/8 teaspoon ascorbic acid (optional)*
- *3 large eggs, beaten*
- *1 cup water, heated to about 80°F*
- *1/4 cup olive oil*
- *2 teaspoons apple cider vinegar*

Instructions:

1. All ingredients should be at room temperature, 70 – 80 F.
2. Set up the bread pan and beater paddle(s). Add wet ingredients first, followed by dry ingredients into the pan.
3. Set aside the yeast in a small bowl. Combine the rest of the dry ingredients in a large mixing bowl, whisking them together thoroughly.
4. Whisk the wet ingredients in a glass measuring cup and pour them into the bread pan. Use a spatula to spread the dry ingredients over the wet mixture, ensuring even coverage. Create a slight well in the center and add the yeast.
5. Place the bread pan in the machine, ensuring it's centered and locked in place. Choose settings: Gluten-free cycle, 1 1/2 pounds loaf, medium crust, then start.
6. About 3 minutes into mixing, open the lid and use a spatula to clear any flour that has collected around the edges and under the dough, avoiding the paddle. Check again during kneading, ensuring all ingredients are well incorporated. Adjust the dough consistency with small amounts of flour blend or warm water if necessary. Keep the lid closed during rise and bake cycles.
7. After baking, check the bread's internal temperature (97°C to 99°C) with an instant-read thermometer. Remove the pan from the machine and place it on a wire cooling rack. Allow the

bread to sit in the pan briefly, then turn the pan upside down to release the loaf. Carefully remove the paddle if it's attached to the bottom. Cool upside down for at least 2 hours before slicing.

8. Store the bread in a resealable plastic bag or airtight container at room temperature for up to 3 days. For longer storage, slice and tightly double-wrap each piece before freezing in a resealable plastic bag for up to 3 months.

Sorghum-Oat Buttermilk Bread

Ingredients

- *4 teaspoons instant yeast*
- *1 1/2 cups sorghum flour (165 g)*
- *1 cup Light Flour Blend (120 g)*
- *1/2 cup gluten-free oat flour (63 g)*
- *1/2 cup buttermilk powder (58 g)*
- *3 tablespoons granulated cane sugar (39 g)*
- *2 teaspoons xanthan gum*
- *2 teaspoons kosher or fine sea salt*
- *1 1/2 teaspoons baking powder*
- *1/2 teaspoon baking soda*
- *1/8 teaspoon ascorbic acid (optional)*
- *2 teaspoons honey*
- *1 cup + 2 tablespoons water, warmed to 80°F (270 ml)*
- *3 large eggs, beaten*
- *1/4 cup olive oil (60 ml)*
- *1 teaspoon apple cider vinegar*

Instructions

1. All ingredients should be at room temperature, 70 – 80 F.
2. Set up the bread pan and beater paddle(s). Add wet ingredients first, followed by dry ingredients into the pan.

3. Set yeast aside in a small bowl. Whisk together the remaining dry ingredients in a large mixing bowl.

4. Dissolve honey in warm water in a glass measuring cup. Add the rest of the wet ingredients and whisk thoroughly. Pour into the bread pan. Spread dry ingredients over the wet mixture, creating a shallow well in the center for the yeast.

5. Place the bread pan in the machine, ensuring it's centered and locked. Choose settings: Gluten-free cycle, 1 1/2 pounds loaf, medium crust, and start.

6. Around 3 minutes into mixing, open the lid and use a spatula to clear any flour on the sides, avoiding the paddle. Check during kneading, scraping edges, corners, and under the dough.

7. Adjust dough consistency with flour blend or warm water if needed. Keep the lid closed during rise and bake cycles.

8. After baking, check the bread's temperature (97°C to 99°C) with a thermometer. Remove the pan and let it rest on a wire rack briefly, then flip to release the loaf. Carefully remove the paddle if attached. Cool upside down for at least 2 hours before slicing.

9. Store the bread in a resealable plastic bag or airtight container at room temperature for up to 3 days. For longer storage, slice, tightly wrap each piece, and freeze in a resealable plastic bag for up to 3 months.

Oat Bread Bliss

Ingredients

- *2 teaspoons instant yeast*
- *240g Light Flour Blend*
- *125g gluten-free oat flour*
- *1/4 cup gluten-free oats or oatmeal*
- *1/4 cup granulated cane sugar*
- *4 teaspoons baking powder*
- *2 teaspoons xanthan gum*
- *1 1/4 teaspoons kosher or fine sea salt*
- *1/8 teaspoon ascorbic acid (optional)*
- *3 large eggs, beaten (at room temperature)*
- *1 cup + 2 tablespoons water (270 ml), warmed to about 80°F (27°C)*

- *1/4 cup olive oil (60 ml)*
- *2 teaspoons apple cider vinegar*
- *Topping:*
- *Water (for brushing)*
- *Gluten-free oats (for sprinkling)*

Instructions

1. All ingredients should be at room temperature, 70 – 80 F.
2. Set up the bread pan and beater paddle(s). Add wet ingredients first, followed by dry ingredients into the pan.
3. Set yeast aside in a small bowl. Whisk together the remaining dry ingredients in a large mixing bowl.
4. Whisk the wet ingredients in a glass measuring cup and pour them into the bread pan. Spread the dry ingredients over the wet mixture, covering it entirely. Create a slight well in the center for the yeast.
5. Place the bread pan in the machine, ensuring it's centered and locked. Choose settings: Gluten-free cycle, 1 1/2 pounds loaf, medium crust, and start.
6. After about 3 minutes of mixing, open the lid and use a spatula to clear any flour on the sides, avoiding the paddle. Check during kneading, scraping edges, corners, and under the dough. Adjust dough consistency with flour blend or warm water if needed. After the mix/knead cycle, brush the loaf's top with water and sprinkle oats. Keep the lid closed during rise and bake cycles.
7. Once baked, check the bread's temperature (97°C to 99°C) with a thermometer. Remove the pan and let it rest on a wire rack briefly, then flip to release the loaf. Carefully remove the paddle if attached. Cool upside down for at least 2 hours before slicing.
8. Store the bread in a resealable plastic bag or airtight container at room temperature for up to 3 days. For longer storage, slice, tightly wrap each piece, and freeze in a resealable plastic bag for up to 3 months.

Walnut Oat Bread

Ingredients

- 2 teaspoons instant yeast
- 2 cups Light Flour Blend
- 1 cup gluten-free oat flour
- 1/2 cup chopped walnuts
- 1/4 cup granulated cane sugar
- 4 teaspoons baking powder
- 2 teaspoons xanthan gum
- 1 1/4 teaspoons kosher or fine sea salt
- 1/8 teaspoon ascorbic acid (optional)
- 3 large eggs, beaten
- 1 cup + 1 tablespoon water (255 ml), warmed to about 80°F (27°C)
- 1/4 cup olive oil (60 ml)
- 2 teaspoons apple cider vinegar
- Topping:
- Water (for brushing)
- Gluten-free oats (for sprinkling)

Instructions

1. All ingredients should be at room temperature, 70 – 80 F.
2. Set up the bread pan and beater paddle(s). Add wet ingredients first, followed by dry ingredients into the pan.
3. Set yeast aside in a small bowl. Whisk the remaining dry ingredients in a large mixing bowl.
4. Combine the wet ingredients in a glass measuring cup and pour them into the bread pan. Spread dry ingredients evenly over the wet mix, creating a slight well in the center for the yeast.
5. Put the bread pan in the machine, center it, and secure it. Select: Gluten-free cycle, 1 1/2 pounds loaf, medium crust, and start.

6. Around 3 minutes into mixing, open the lid and use a spatula to clear any flour on the sides, avoiding the paddle. Check during kneading, scraping edges, corners, and under the dough. Adjust dough consistency with flour blend or warm water if needed.

7. Once kneading is done, delicately brush the loaf top with water, sprinkle oats, gently pressing them onto the dough. Keep the lid closed during rise and bake cycles.

8. After baking, ensure the bread reaches 97°C to 99°C (97°C to 99°C) with a thermometer. Remove the pan and rest it on a wire rack briefly. Flip to release the loaf. Carefully remove the paddle if attached. Cool upside down for at least 2 hours before slicing.

9. Store the bread in a resealable plastic bag or airtight container at room temperature for up to 3 days. For longer storage, slice, tightly wrap each piece, and freeze in a resealable plastic bag for up to 3 months.

Seeded Bagels Recipe

Ingredients

- *1 tablespoon instant yeast*
- *2 cups Light Flour Blend or Whole-Grain Flour Blend*
- *1/2 cup teff flour*
- *1/2 cup millet flour*
- *1/3 cup tapioca starch*
- *2 tablespoons flaxseed meal or ground flaxseed*
- *1 teaspoon kosher salt*
- *3/4 teaspoon xanthan gum or psyllium husk flakes or powder*
- *1/2 teaspoon dough enhancer*
- *2 tablespoons honey*
- *1 cup water, warmed to about 80°F (27°C)*
- *1 large egg, at room temperature, beaten*
- *2 tablespoons vegetable oil*
- *2 teaspoons cider vinegar*
- *Baking Soda Wash:*
- *1/4 teaspoon baking soda*
- *1 cup warm water*

Topping:

- *2 tablespoons poppy seeds*
- *2 tablespoons white sesame seeds*
- *1 tablespoon sunflower seeds*
- *1 tablespoon flaxseed meal or ground flaxseed*
- *1 teaspoon kosher salt*

Instructions:

1. All ingredients should be at room temperature, 70 – 80 F.
2. Place parchment paper on a baking sheet.
3. Set up the bread pan and beater paddle(s). Add wet ingredients first, followed by dry ingredients into the pan.
4. Place yeast in a small bowl aside. Mix all remaining dry ingredients in a large bowl.
5. In a 2-cup (0.5 liter) glass measuring cup, whisk honey and water until honey dissolves. Add other wet ingredients, then pour into the bread pan. Spread dry ingredients over the wet mix, making a shallow well in the center for the yeast.
6. Put the bread pan in the machine, ensuring it's centered and locked. Select Dough cycle - Loaf size: 1 1/2 pounds/750 g - Start.
7. After the first kneading cycle, scrape the sides and bottom to ensure all dry ingredients mix well. Once the cycle finishes, take out the dough and divide it into eight pieces on a lightly oiled surface.
8. Whisk baking soda into warm water in a 2-cup measuring cup.
9. Shape each dough piece into a 6-inch (15 cm) log, then form circles, sealing the ends. Place them on the baking sheet and brush with the baking soda wash.
10. Combine all topping ingredients, sprinkle over the bagels, and lightly press for seed adhesion. Cover with oiled plastic wrap, and let rise for 1 hour; they'll puff up but not double in size.
11. Preheat oven to 400°F (200°C) while the bagels rise.
12. Bake for 25-30 minutes until golden brown.
13. Store in a resealable plastic bag or airtight container on the counter for up to 2 days. For longer storage, double-wrap tightly in plastic, place in a resealable plastic bag, and freeze for up to 3 months.

Wholesome Pretzel Rounds

Ingredients

For the Dough:

- *2 tablespoons instant yeast (about 21g)*
- *3 cups Light Flour Blend or Whole-Grain Flour Blend (approximately 360g)*
- *3/4 cup cornstarch, potato starch, or arrowroot (around 96g)*
- *2 1/2 teaspoons kosher or fine sea salt*
- *2 teaspoons psyllium husk flakes or powder*
- *3/4 teaspoon baking powder*
- *Optional: 1/8 teaspoon ascorbic acid*

For the Wet Mix:

- *1 teaspoon honey*
- *1 1/4 cups warm water (about 300ml)*
- *2 large egg whites at room temperature*
- *2 teaspoons apple cider vinegar*
- *For the Baking Soda Wash:*
- *1 cup water (240ml)*
- *1/4 teaspoon baking soda*

For Topping:

- *1 large egg yolk*
- *2 teaspoons water*
- *Pretzel salt or coarse-flaked salt*

Instructions

1. All ingredients should be at room temperature, 70 – 80 F.
2. Grab a baking sheet, line it with parchment paper, and give it a light brush of oil. Don't forget to do the same for a muffin pan - either a 6-cup jumbo or a 12-cup regular one.

3. Set up the bread pan and beater paddle(s). Add wet ingredients first, followed by dry ingredients into the pan.

4. Start by dissolving the yeast in a small bowl. In another bowl, whisk all the remaining dry ingredients together.

5. Mix the honey and warm water in a glass measuring cup until the honey is dissolved. Add the rest of the wet ingredients and give it another whisk. Pour this into the bread pan, layer the dry ingredients over it, make a shallow well, and add the yeast.

6. Place the bread pan into the machine and set it to the Dough cycle for a 1 1/2 pound/750g loaf. Hit start.

7. Let the machine work its magic, making sure to scrape down any flour sticking to the sides or under the dough until everything's mixed well. It should take about 5 minutes for a smooth, lump-free dough. Stop the cycle and turn off the machine.

8. Take out the dough, scoop it onto the baking sheet, lightly oil the top, and flatten it into a disk. For larger rolls, split the dough into six equal pieces; for smaller ones, go for twelve.

9. Oil your hands slightly, roll each piece into a ball, and place them in the muffin pan cups. Cover them with oiled plastic wrap, then let them rise in a warm part of your kitchen for around 1 1/2 hours. They won't double but will puff up.

10. While they rise, preheat your oven to 350°F (180°C) and position a rack in the center.

11. When the rolls are nearly done rising, mix water and baking soda in a saucepan. Heat it until boiling while stirring occasionally. Remove from heat.

12. Whisk the egg yolk and water together. This mixture will help the salt stick and give the rolls a beautiful golden hue.

13. Gently brush each ball of dough with the baking soda wash using a pastry brush. Let it sit for a minute, then brush the entire top with the beaten egg. Sprinkle salt on each roll and score an X on top with a sharp knife.

14. Bake until deep brown and check with a thermometer to ensure they're around 210°F (99°C). Larger rolls will take about 50 to 60 minutes, while smaller ones around 35 minutes or until golden.

15. After 2 minutes in the pan, transfer the rolls to a wire rack to cool. This allows steam to escape, keeping the outside crunchy. Let them cool for at least 20 minutes before serving.

They're best on the day they're made but if you have leftovers, pop them in the oven for a few minutes the next day to freshen and crisp them up.

Heavenly Polish Babka

Ingredients

For the Babka

- *1 tablespoon instant yeast*
- *2 1/2 cups Light Flour Blend or Whole-Grain Flour Blend (about 300g)*
- *1/4 cup granulated cane sugar (around 48g)*
- *1 tablespoon psyllium husk flakes or powder*
- *2 teaspoons baking powder*
- *1 teaspoon dough enhancer*
- *1/2 teaspoon kosher salt*
- *1/4 cup golden raisins (about 35g)*
- *1/4 cup chopped mixed dried fruit or candied citron (about 35g)*
- *1/2 cup unsweetened coconut milk (about 120ml)*
- *3 large eggs, beaten*
- *1/2 stick non-dairy butter substitute, melted and slightly cooled (around 56g)*
- *2 teaspoons apple cider vinegar*

Rum Syrup:

- *1/2 cup granulated cane sugar (about 100g)*
- *1/4 cup water (around 60ml)*
- *1 to 2 tablespoons rum (dark or light, your choice)*

Instructions

1. All ingredients should be at room temperature, 70 – 80 F.
2. Set up the bread pan and beater paddle(s). Add wet ingredients first, followed by dry ingredients into the pan.

3. Your yeast takes a small bowl detour. Meanwhile, in a large mixing bowl, whisk together the flour blend, sugar, psyllium husk, baking powder, dough enhancer, and salt. Toss in those delightful raisins and mixed dried fruit. Set this bowl of goodness aside.

4. In a 2-cup glass measuring cup, whisk your wet ingredients together and pour this into the bread pan. Use a spatula to cover those liquids with the dry ingredients, making a cozy well in the middle for the yeast.

5. Pop the bread pan into the machine, locking it securely, and set it to the Dough cycle for a 1 1/2 pound/750g loaf. Let the magic start.

6. While the machine works its kneading magic, peek inside occasionally. Use a spatula to scrape down any stray flour clinging to the sides or under the dough, ensuring everything's beautifully mixed. It should take around 5 minutes to get that perfect, lump-free dough. Stop the cycle, turn off the machine, and liberate the pan.

7. Now, it's Bundt pan time! Oil up that 10-cup Bundt pan and transfer the dough there. Cover the pan with an oiled sheet of plastic wrap, oil-side down, and let that dough rest for 30 to 45 minutes.

8. Get the oven preheated to a cozy 350°F (180°C). It's baking time! Slide the babka into the oven and let it bake for 35 to 40 minutes until your thermometer declares it's at least 190°F (88°C).

9. While your babka becomes golden perfection, summon the rum syrup in a small saucepan. Let the sugar dissolve in water over medium-high heat, add in the rum, and bring it to a lovely boil. Remove it from the heat.

10. When your babka emerges beautifully baked, resting in its pan, take a toothpick or fork and gently poke it all over. Pour that delicious rum syrup slowly over the surface. Let it soak up for about 30 minutes. After the absorption dance, turn the babka out onto a rack and let it cool for an hour before slicing.

11. Keep this divine creation in a resealable bag or airtight container on your counter for up to 3 days. Want it to last longer? Slice it evenly, double-wrap each slice snugly in plastic, bag them up, and freeze for up to 3 months.

Optional: Whisk together 1 cup of confectioners' sugar, 2 tablespoons of nondairy milk, and a pinch of salt until smooth. Once your babka cools, let that glaze drizzle over it.

Spicy Southwest Chile-Cheese Bread

Ingredients

- *For the Bread:*
- *2 teaspoons instant yeast*
- *3 cups Light Flour Blend (360g)*
- *1/4 cup granulated cane sugar (about 48g)*
- *1 tablespoon baking powder*
- *2 teaspoons xanthan gum*
- *1 teaspoon kosher salt*
- *Optional: 1/8 teaspoon ascorbic acid*
- *1/2 cup grated chipotle Havarti, pepper jack, or chile-infused cheese (about 56g)*
- *1 cup + 3 tablespoons 1% milk or water, heated to around 80°F (27°C) (about 285ml)*
- *3 large eggs, beaten*
- *1/4 cup olive oil (about 60ml)*
- *2 teaspoons apple cider vinegar*
- *1 teaspoon hot green chili oil*

Instructions

1. All ingredients should be at room temperature, 70 – 80 F.
2. Set up the bread pan and beater paddle(s). Add wet ingredients first, followed by dry ingredients into the pan.
3. Your yeast gets its small bowl to chill. Meanwhile, whisk the rest of the dry ingredients in a large mixing bowl, but hold off on adding that tantalizing cheese just yet. Once combined, toss in the cheese, making sure it's evenly spread throughout.
4. In a glass measuring cup, whisk together the wet ingredients and pour this delightful mix into the bread pan. Use a spatula to ensure the dry ingredients are covering the wet completely. Create a cozy well in the middle and pour in the yeast.
5. Into the machine, the bread pan goes, snugly settled and securely locked. Select the Gluten-free cycle, a 1 1/2 pound/750g loaf size, and opt for a Medium crust. Let the magic begin with the push of the Start button.

6. About 3 minutes into this mixing frenzy, peek inside. Use a spatula to scrape down any clingy flour from the sides, avoiding the paddle. Repeat this beauty check during kneading, ensuring everything's well-blended. Adjust with tiny flour or water doses if needed. Then, let the machine work its rise and bake cycles without interference.

7. At the bake cycle's end, lift the lid and employ your trusty instant-read thermometer. When that bread hits 97°C to 99°C (97°C to 99°C) in the center, it's perfection! Remove the pan from the machine, let it rest on a wire rack for a couple of minutes, then turn it upside down to slide the loaf onto the rack. Gently remove the paddle if it's sticking around and let the bread cool upside down for a solid 2 hours before slicing.

8. Keep this spicy delight in a resealable bag or airtight container on your counter for up to 3 days. Want it to last longer? Slice it evenly, double-wrap each slice securely in plastic, bag them up, and freeze for up to 3 months.

Asiago Bread Recipe

Ingredients

- *2 teaspoons instant yeast*
- *240 g Light Flour Blend*
- *110 g sorghum flour*
- *44 g milk powder*
- *26 g flaxseed meal or ground flaxseed*
- *39 g granulated cane sugar*
- *1 tbsp baking powder*
- *2 tsp xanthan gum*
- *1 1/2 tsp kosher or fine sea salt*
- *1/8 tsp ascorbic acid*
- *50 g shredded Asiago cheese*
- *3 large eggs, beaten (at room temperature)*
- *270 ml water, warmed to about 80°F (27°C)*
- *45 ml olive oil*
- *2 tsp apple cider vinegar*
- *Toppings:*

- *25 g shredded Asiago cheese*
- *1 tbsp minced fresh parsley*

Instructions

1. All ingredients should be at room temperature, 70 – 80 F.

2. Set up the bread pan and beater paddle(s). Add wet ingredients first, followed by dry ingredients into the pan.

3. Set the yeast aside in a small bowl. In a large mixing bowl, combine the remaining dry ingredients (except the cheese). Then, add the cheese and mix it evenly through the dry ingredients.

4. Whisk the wet ingredients in a glass measuring cup. Pour the wet mixture into the bread pan. Spread the dry ingredients over the wet ones, making a shallow well in the center for the yeast.

5. Put the bread pan in the machine, ensuring it's centered and locked. Close the lid and select the Gluten-free cycle, Loaf size: 1 1/2 pounds/750 g, and Medium crust. Start the cycle.

6. Around 3 minutes into mixing, open the lid and use a spatula to scrape down the sides of the pan. Check the dough's consistency a couple of times during kneading and adjust by adding a bit of flour blend or warm water if necessary.

7. After the mix/knead cycle, sprinkle the shredded cheese and parsley over the top. Close the lid for the remaining rise and bake cycles.

8. Once baked, check the bread's temperature (97°C to 99°C or 97°C to 99°C) with an instant-read thermometer. Remove the pan from the machine, let it rest on a wire rack for a few minutes, then transfer the loaf onto the rack to cool for at least 2 hours before slicing.

9. Store the bread in a resealable airtight container on your counter for up to 3 days. For longer storage, slice it evenly, wrap it tightly in plastic, place it in a resealable plastic bag, and freeze it for up to 3 months.

Blue Cheese and Walnut Bread Recipe

Ingredients

- *2 teaspoons instant yeast*
- *240 g Light Flour Blend*
- *120 g teff flour*

- *44 g Better Than Milk Soy powder*
- *39 g granulated cane sugar*
- *1 tbsp baking powder*
- *2 tsp xanthan gum*
- *1 tsp kosher or fine sea salt*
- *1/8 tsp ascorbic acid (optional)*
- *3 large eggs, beaten*
- *240 ml water, warmed to about 80°F (27°C)*
- *45 ml vegetable oil*
- *2 tsp apple cider vinegar*
- *90 g crumbled blue cheese*
- *120 g chopped toasted walnuts*

Instructions

1. All ingredients should be at room temperature, 70 – 80 F.
2. Set up the bread pan and beater paddle(s). Add wet ingredients first, followed by dry ingredients into the pan.
3. Reserve the yeast in a small bowl. Whisk together the remaining dry ingredients (except the blue cheese) in a large mixing bowl.
4. Whisk the wet ingredients (excluding blue cheese) in a glass measuring cup and pour into the bread pan. Scatter the crumbled blue cheese on top. Spread the dry ingredients evenly over the wet ones, creating a well in the center for the yeast.
5. Put the bread pan in the machine, ensuring it's centered and locked. Close the lid and select the Gluten-free cycle, Loaf size: 1 1/2 pounds/750 g, and Medium crust. Start the cycle.
6. About 3 minutes into mixing, open the lid and use a spatula to scrape down the sides of the pan. Check the dough's consistency during kneading, adjusting by adding a bit of flour blend or warm water if needed.
7. Once the initial kneading is done, add the chopped toasted walnuts. Allow the machine to complete the mixing and kneading cycles without opening the lid.
8. When the bake cycle ends, check the bread's temperature (97°C to 99°C or 97°C to 99°C) using an instant-read thermometer inserted in the center. Once done, remove the pan from the

machine and place it on a wire rack. Let the bread sit in the pan for a few minutes, then invert it onto the rack to cool upside down for at least 2 hours before slicing.

9. Store the bread on the counter for up to 3 days in a resealable plastic bag or an airtight container. For longer storage, slice it evenly, wrap it tightly in plastic, place it in a resealable plastic bag, and freeze it for u to 3 months.

Chorizo and Cheddar Cornbread Recipe

Ingredients

- *170 g Mexican chorizo, crumbled and cooked until browned, then drained and cooled.*
- *2 teaspoons instant yeast*
- *240 g Light Flour Blend*
- *156 g corn flour*
- *26 g granulated cane sugar*
- *1 tbsp baking powder*
- *1 tsp kosher salt*
- *1 tsp xanthan gum*
- *1/4 cup vegetable oil or unsalted melted butter (60 ml or 55 g)*
- *3 large eggs, beaten (at room temperature)*
- *180 ml water, warmed to about 80°F (27°C)*
- *2 tsp apple cider vinegar*
- *84 g shredded cheddar cheese*

Instructions

1. Cook the crumbled chorizo in a skillet over medium heat until browned (about 8 minutes). Drain thoroughly on paper towels and let it cool.
2. All ingredients should be at room temperature, 70 – 80 F.
3. Set up the bread pan and beater paddle(s). Add wet ingredients first, followed by dry ingredients into the pan.
4. Keep the yeast aside in a small bowl. In a large mixing bowl, combine the remaining dry ingredients with the cooked chorizo, setting the bowl aside.

5. In a glass measuring cup, whisk together the wet ingredients (excluding the cheese). Stir in the shredded cheddar cheese and pour this mixture into the bread pan. Spread the dry ingredients evenly over the wet ones, creating a well in the center for the yeast.

6. Place the bread pan in the machine, ensuring it's centered and locked. Close the lid and select the Gluten-free cycle, Loaf size: 1 1/2 pounds/750 g, and Medium crust. Start the cycle.

7. Around 3 minutes into mixing, open the lid and scrape down the sides of the pan using a spatula. Check the dough's consistency during kneading, adding a little flour blend or warm water if necessary.

8. At the end of the bake cycle, verify the bread's internal temperature (97°C to 99°C or 97°C to 99°C) using an instant-read thermometer inserted into the center. Once done, remove the pan from the machine, let it sit for a few minutes, then invert it onto a wire rack to cool upside down for at least 2 hours before slicing.

9. Store the bread on the counter for up to 3 days in a resealable plastic bag or an airtight container. For longer storage, slice it evenly, wrap it tightly in plastic, place it in a resealable plastic bag, and freeze it for up to 3 months.

Scallion and Cilantro Cornbread Recipe

Ingredients

- 240 g Light Flour Blend
- 104 g corn flour
- 48 g granulated cane sugar
- 1 tbsp baking powder
- 1 tsp kosher salt
- 1 tsp xanthan gum or psyllium husk flakes or powder
- 1/4 cup vegetable oil or melted nondairy butter substitute (60 ml or 55 g)
- 3 large eggs, beaten (at room temperature)
- 240 ml water, warmed to about 80°F (27°C)
- 2 scallions, finely chopped
- 1 tbsp finely chopped fresh cilantro

Instructions

1. All ingredients should be at room temperature, 70 – 80 F.

2. Set up the bread pan and beater paddle(s). Add wet ingredients first, followed by dry ingredients into the pan.

3. Whisk together all of the dry ingredients in a large mixing bowl. Whisk the wet ingredients together in a glass measuring cup. Pour this wet mixture into the bread pan and spread the dry ingredients evenly over the wet ones.

4. Place the bread pan in the machine, ensuring it's centered and locked. Close the lid and select the Quick bread/cake cycle, Loaf size: 1 1/2 pounds/750 g, and Medium crust. Start the cycle.

5. Around 3 minutes into mixing, open the lid and use a spatula to scrape down the sides of the pan. Check the dough's consistency during kneading, adjusting with a little flour blend or warm water if needed. Add the chopped scallions and cilantro during this step. If your machine allows, remove the paddle before the baking cycle.

6. At the end of the bake cycle, check the bread's internal temperature using an instant-read thermometer (97°C to 99°C or 97°C to 99°C). Once done, remove the pan from the machine and place it on a wire rack. Let the bread sit for a couple of minutes, then invert the pan to release the loaf onto the wire rack. If there's a paddle embedded, remove it carefully. Allow the bread to cool upside down for at least 2 hours before slicing.

7. Store the bread on the counter for up to 3 days in a resealable plastic bag or an airtight container. For longer storage, slice it evenly, wrap it tightly in plastic, place it in a resealable plastic bag, and freeze it for up to 3 months.

Jalapeño-Cheese Cornbread Recipe

Ingredients:

- 2 teaspoons instant yeast
- 240 g Light Flour Blend
- 156 g corn flour
- 39 g granulated cane sugar
- 2 tsp baking powder
- 1 tsp kosher or fine sea salt
- 1 tsp psyllium husk flakes or powder

- Wet Ingredients:
- 1/3 cup vegetable oil or melted unsalted butter (80 ml or 75 g)
- 3 large eggs, beaten (at room temperature)
- 180 ml water, warmed to about 80°F (27°C)
- 2 tsp apple cider vinegar
- 84 g shredded Colby or cheddar jack cheese or dairy-free substitute (such as Daiya brand)
- 135 g pickled jalapeños, finely chopped

Instructions:

1. All ingredients should be at room temperature, 70 – 80 F.
2. Set up the bread pan and beater paddle(s). Add wet ingredients first, followed by dry ingredients into the pan.
3. Set the yeast aside in a small bowl. Whisk together all of the dry ingredients in a large mixing bowl. In a glass measuring cup, whisk together the wet ingredients except for the cheese and jalapeños. Stir in the shredded cheese and chopped jalapeños, and pour this mixture into the bread pan. Spread the dry ingredients evenly over the wet mix, creating a shallow well in the center for the yeast.
4. Place the bread pan in the machine, ensuring it's centered and locked. Close the lid and select the Gluten-free cycle, Loaf size: 1 1/2 pounds/750 g, and Light crust. Start the cycle.
5. About 3 minutes into the mixing process, open the lid and use a spatula to scrape down the sides of the pan, ensuring even mixing. Check the dough's consistency during kneading and adjust by adding a little flour blend or warm water if necessary.
6. When the bake cycle finishes, check the bread's internal temperature using an instant-read thermometer (97°C to 99°C or 97°C to 99°C). Once done, remove the pan from the machine and transfer it onto a wire rack. Allow the bread to sit for a few minutes, then invert the pan to release the loaf onto the wire rack. If there's a paddle embedded, carefully remove it. Let the bread cool upside down for at least 2 hours before slicing.
7. Store the bread on the counter for up to 3 days in a resealable plastic bag or an airtight container. For longer storage, slice it evenly, wrap it tightly in plastic, place it in a resealable plastic bag, and freeze it for up to 3 months.

Note: Cornmeal and corn flour vary in texture; corn flour is finely ground compared to cornmeal.

Fresh Rosemary Bread Recipe

Ingredients

- *2 teaspoons instant yeast*
- *360 g Light Flour Blend*
- *1/2 cup milk powder (44 g) or DariFree (69 g)*
- *48 g granulated cane sugar*
- *1 heaping tablespoon minced fresh rosemary*
- *1 tablespoon baking powder*
- *2 teaspoons xanthan gum*
- *2 teaspoons kosher salt*
- *1/8 teaspoon ascorbic acid (optional)*
- *3 large eggs, beaten (at room temperature)*
- *285 ml water, warmed to about 80°F (27°C)*
- *60 ml olive oil*
- *2 teaspoons apple cider vinegar*

Instructions

1. All ingredients should be at room temperature, 70 – 80 F.
2. Set up the bread pan and beater paddle(s). Add wet ingredients first, followed by dry ingredients into the pan.
3. Keep the yeast aside in a small bowl. Whisk together all of the dry ingredients in a large mixing bowl.
4. In a glass measuring cup, whisk together the wet ingredients and pour them into the bread pan. Use a spatula to cover the wet ingredients completely with the dry mix, making a shallow well in the center for the yeast.
5. Place the bread pan in the machine, ensuring it's centered and secured. Close the lid and select the Gluten-free cycle, Loaf size: 1 1/2 pounds/750 g, and Medium crust. Start the cycle.
6. About 3 minutes into the mixing process, open the lid and use a spatula to scrape down the sides of the pan, ensuring even mixing. Check the dough's consistency during kneading,

adjusting with a bit of flour blend or warm water if needed. Once the mix/knead cycle ends, keep the lid closed for rising and baking.

7. When the bake cycle finishes, check the bread's internal temperature (97°C to 99°C or 97°C to 99°C). Remove the pan from the machine and place it on a wire rack. After a couple of minutes, invert the pan to release the loaf onto the wire rack. Carefully remove the paddle if attached. Let the bread cool upside down for at least 2 hours before slicing.

8. Store the bread in a resealable plastic bag or an airtight container on the counter for up to 3 days. For longer storage, slice it evenly, tightly wrap each slice in plastic, place them in a resealable plastic bag, and freeze for up to 3 months.

Lemon-Thyme Bread Recipe

Ingredients

- *2 teaspoons instant yeast*
- *360 g Light Flour Blend*
- *58 g buttermilk powder*
- *39 g granulated cane sugar*
- *1 tablespoon baking powder*
- *1 tablespoon fresh thyme leaves*
- *2 teaspoons xanthan gum*
- *2 teaspoons kosher or fine sea salt*
- *1/8 teaspoon ascorbic acid (optional)*
- *56 g unsalted butter, melted and slightly cooled*
- *3 large eggs, beaten (at room temperature)*
- *240 ml water, warmed to about 80°F (27°C)*
- *1 1/2 teaspoons very finely grated lemon zest*
- *1 teaspoon apple cider vinegar*

Instructions

1. All ingredients should be at room temperature, 70 – 80 F.
2. Set up the bread pan and beater paddle(s). Add wet ingredients first, followed by dry ingredients into the pan.

3. Set aside the yeast in a small bowl. Whisk together all of the dry ingredients in a large mixing bowl.

4. Whisk the wet ingredients together in a glass measuring cup and pour them into the bread pan. Use a spatula to cover the wet ingredients completely with the dry mix, creating a shallow well in the center for the yeast.

5. Put the bread pan in the machine, ensuring it's centered and secured. Close the lid and select the Gluten-free cycle, Loaf size: 1 1/2 pounds/750 g, and Medium crust. Start the cycle.

6. About 3 minutes into the mixing process, open the lid and use a spatula to scrape down the sides of the pan, ensuring even mixing. Adjust the dough consistency if needed by adding a bit of flour blend or warm water. After the mix/knead cycle, keep the lid closed for rising and baking. For the lemon zest, use a fine grater.

7. Once the bake cycle finishes, check the bread's internal temperature (97°C to 99°C or 97°C to 99°C). Remove the pan from the machine and place it on a wire rack. After a couple of minutes, invert the pan to release the loaf onto the wire rack. Carefully remove the paddle if attached. Let the bread cool upside down for at least 2 hours before slicing.

8. Store the bread in a resealable plastic bag or an airtight container on the counter for up to 3 days. For longer storage, slice it evenly, tightly wrap each slice in plastic, place them in a resealable plastic bag, and freeze for up to 3 months.

9. Note: To evenly disperse citrus zests in recipes, add them to the liquid ingredients.

Mexican Salsa Bread Recipe

Ingredients

- *2 teaspoons instant yeast*
- *360 g Light Flour Blend*
- *30 g corn flour*
- *48 g granulated cane sugar*
- *1 tablespoon baking powder*
- *1 tablespoon chopped fresh cilantro*
- *2 1/2 teaspoons tomato powder*
- *2 teaspoons xanthan gum*
- *1 teaspoon red pepper flakes (adjust to taste accordingly)*

- *1 teaspoon onion powder*
- *1 teaspoon kosher salt*
- *1/8 teaspoon ascorbic acid (optional)*
- *3 large eggs, beaten*
- *285 ml water, warmed to about 80°F (27°C)*
- *60 ml olive oil*
- *2 teaspoons apple cider vinegar*

Instructions

1. All ingredients should be at room temperature, 70 – 80 F.
2. Set up the bread pan and beater paddle(s). Add wet ingredients first, followed by dry ingredients into the pan.
3. Set aside the yeast in a small bowl. Whisk together all of the dry ingredients in a large mixing bowl.
4. Whisk the wet ingredients together in a glass measuring cup and pour them into the bread pan. Use a spatula to cover the wet ingredients completely with the dry mix, creating a shallow well in the center for the yeast.
5. Put the bread pan in the machine, ensuring it's centered and secured. Close the lid and select the Gluten-free cycle, Loaf size: 1 1/2 pounds/750 g, and Medium crust. Start the cycle.
6. About 3 minutes into the mixing process, open the lid and use a spatula to scrape down the sides of the pan, ensuring even mixing. Adjust the dough consistency if needed by adding a bit of flour blend or warm water. Once the mix/knead cycle is done, leave the lid closed for rising and baking.
7. Once the bake cycle finishes, check the bread's internal temperature (97°C to 99°C or 97°C to 99°C). Remove the pan from the machine and place it on a wire rack. After a couple of minutes, invert the pan to release the loaf onto the wire rack. Carefully remove the paddle if attached. Let the bread cool upside down for at least 2 hours before slicing.
8. Store the bread in a resealable plastic bag or an airtight container on the counter for up to 3 days. For longer storage, slice it evenly, tightly wrap each slice in plastic, place them in a resealable plastic bag, and freeze for up to 3 months.

Pizza Pie Bread Recipe

Ingredients

- *2 teaspoons instant yeast*
- *360 g Light Flour Blend*
- *44 g milk powder*
- *39 g granulated cane sugar*
- *2 tbsp Parmesan cheese, finely grated, or powdered cheddar cheese*
- *1 tablespoon baking powder*
- *1 tablespoon dried oregano*
- *2 teaspoons xanthan gum*
- *2 teaspoons kosher salt*
- *2 teaspoons dried basil*
- *1 1/2 teaspoons onion powder*
- *1 1/2 teaspoons tomato powder*
- *1/4 teaspoon garlic powder*
- *1/8 teaspoon ascorbic acid (optional)*
- *3 large eggs, beaten*
- *270 ml water, warmed to about 80°F (27°C)*
- *60 ml olive oil*
- *2 teaspoons apple cider vinegar*

Instructions

1. All ingredients should be at room temperature, 70 – 80 F.
2. Set up the bread pan and beater paddle(s). Add wet ingredients first, followed by dry ingredients into the pan.
3. Set aside the yeast in a small bowl. In a separate large mixing bowl, combine the remaining dry ingredients.
4. Whisk together the wet ingredients in a glass measuring cup and pour them into the bread pan. Use a spatula to cover the wet ingredients completely with the dry mix, creating a shallow well in the center for the yeast.

5. Place the bread pan in the machine and ensure it's centered and locked. Select the Gluten-free cycle, Loaf size: 1 1/2 pounds/750 g, and Medium crust. Start the cycle.

6. After 3 minutes into the mixing process, open the lid and scrape down the sides of the pan. Adjust the dough consistency if needed by adding a bit of flour blend or warm water. Then, leave the lid closed for the remaining rise and bake cycles.

7. Once the bake cycle finishes, check the bread's internal temperature (97°C to 99°C or 97°C to 99°C). Remove the pan from the machine and place it on a wire rack. After a couple of minutes, invert the pan to release the loaf onto the wire rack. Carefully remove the paddle if attached. Let the bread cool upside down for at least 2 hours before slicing.

8. Store the bread in a resealable plastic bag or an airtight container on the counter for up to 3 days. For longer storage, slice it evenly, tightly wrap each slice in plastic, place them in a resealable plastic bag, and freeze for up to 3 months.

Sweet Cornbread

Ingredients

- *172g corn flour*
- *120g Light Flour Blend*
- *60g millet flour*
- *200g granulated cane sugar*
- *1 tablespoon baking powder*
- *1 teaspoon kosher or fine sea salt*
- *1 teaspoon xanthan gum or psyllium husk flakes/powder*
- *1/3 cup vegetable oil or nondairy butter substitute, melted and slightly cooled*
- *240 ml unsweetened soy or coconut milk*
- *3 large eggs, beaten*

Instructions

1. All ingredients should be at room temperature, 70 – 80 F.
2. Set up the bread pan and beater paddle(s). Add wet ingredients first, followed by dry ingredients into the pan.
3. Whisk the dry ingredients together in a large mixing bowl.

4. In a 2-cup glass measuring cup, whisk the wet ingredients together and pour them into the bread pan. Use a spatula to ensure the dry ingredients cover the wet ingredients completely.

5. Place the bread pan in the machine, settle it in the center, and lock it. Select the Quick bread/cake cycle, Loaf size: 1 1/2 pounds/750 g, and Light crust. Start the cycle.

6. After the initial kneading cycle, check the dough's consistency. Scrape the sides and bottom of the pan to incorporate any remaining dry ingredients. If needed, reshape the loaf or remove the paddle if your machine allows.

7. Let the bread finish baking undisturbed until the cycle ends.

8. Check the bread's internal temperature (97°C to 99°C or 97°C to 99°C) using an instant-read thermometer inserted into the center of the loaf. Remove the pan from the machine and let the bread cool on a wire rack for a couple of minutes. Then, transfer the loaf onto the wire rack to cool sideways. Allow it to cool for at least 2 hours before slicing.

9. Store the bread in a resealable plastic bag or an airtight container on the counter for up to 3 days. For longer storage, slice it, tightly wrap each slice in plastic, place it in a resealable plastic bag, and freeze it for up to 3 months.

Irish Soda Bread

Ingredients

- *2 teaspoons instant yeast*
- *180 g Light Flour Blend or Whole-Grain Flour Blend*
- *120 g sorghum flour*
- *60 g potato starch (not potato flour)*
- *26 g granulated cane sugar*
- *1 tablespoon baking powder*
- *2 teaspoons psyllium husk flakes or powder*
- *2 teaspoons baking soda*
- *1 teaspoon kosher or fine sea salt*
- *1/8 teaspoon ascorbic acid (optional)*
- *59 ml non-dairy butter substitute, melted and slightly cooled*
- *350 ml unsweetened soy or coconut milk*
- *1 tablespoon apple cider vinegar*

- *1 tablespoon freshly squeezed lemon juice*
- *Add-in:*
- *1 cup dried currants*

Instructions:

1. All ingredients should be at room temperature, 70 – 80 F.
2. Set up the bread pan and beater paddle(s). Add wet ingredients first, followed by dry ingredients into the pan.
3. Whisk the remaining dry ingredients together in a large mixing bowl.
9. In a 2-cup glass measuring cup, whisk the wet ingredients together and pour them into the bread pan. Use a spatula to ensure the dry ingredients cover the wet ingredients completely, creating a shallow well in the center for the yeast.
4. Place the bread pan in the machine, settle it in the center, and lock it. Select the Gluten-free cycle, Loaf size: 1 1/2 pounds/750 g, and Light crust. Start the cycle.
5. After the initial kneading cycle, incorporate the dried currants into the dough by carefully adding them. If your machine allows, remove the paddle when it transitions from kneading to rise. If needed, reshape the loaf or smooth the top of the dough.
6. Allow the bread machine to complete the rise and bake cycles without opening the lid.
7. Check the bread's internal temperature (97°C to 99°C or 97°C to 99°C) using an instant-read thermometer inserted into the center of the loaf. Remove the pan from the machine and let the bread cool in the pan for 3 minutes. Then, remove the loaf from the pan and let it cool sideways on a wire rack for at least 1 hour before slicing.
8. Store the bread in a resealable plastic bag or an airtight container on the counter for up to 3 days. For longer storage, slice the bread, tightly wrap each slice in plastic, place them in a resealable plastic bag, and freeze for up to 3 months.

Portuguese Sweet Bread

Ingredients

- *2 teaspoons instant yeast*
- *360 g Light Flour Blend*
- *48 g granulated cane sugar*

- *1 tablespoon baking powder*
- *2 teaspoons xanthan gum*
- *1 teaspoon kosher salt*
- *Wet Ingredients:*
- *60 g honey*
- *255 ml water, warmed to about 80°F (27°C)*
- *56 g non-dairy butter substitute, melted and slightly cooled*
- *2 large eggs, at room temperature*
- *2 teaspoons apple cider vinegar*

Instructions:

1. All ingredients should be at room temperature, 70 – 80 F.
2. Set up the bread pan and beater paddle(s). Add wet ingredients first, followed by dry ingredients into the pan.
3. Whisk the yeast in a small bowl and set it aside. Whisk the remaining dry ingredients together in a large mixing bowl.
4. In a glass measuring cup, whisk together the honey and warm water to dissolve the honey. Add the remaining wet ingredients, then pour this mixture into the bread pan. Spread the dry ingredients over the wet ones, ensuring they're completely covered, creating a shallow well in the center for the yeast.
5. Place the bread pan in the machine, ensuring it's settled in the center and locked in place. Select the Gluten-free cycle, Loaf size: 1 1/2 pounds/750 g, and Medium crust setting. Start the cycle.
6. During mixing, check after a few minutes to scrape down the sides of the pan, avoiding the paddle. Adjust the dough consistency if needed by adding a little flour blend or warm water, as required.
7. Let the bread machine complete the rise and bake cycles without opening the lid. The bread should rise to about 1/2 inch (1 cm) below the bread pan's level and then settle, flattening the top.
8. Check the bread's internal temperature (97°C to 99°C or 97°C to 99°C) with an instant-read thermometer to confirm it's done. Once baked, remove the bread pan from the machine and let it cool on a wire rack. Carefully remove the paddle if it's embedded in the loaf.

9. Allow the bread to cool sideways for at least 2 hours before slicing. Store it in a resealable plastic bag or airtight container on the counter for up to 3 days. For longer storage, slice and tightly wrap individual slices in plastic, place them in a resealable plastic bag, and freeze them for up to 3 months.

Walnut-Cranberry Oat Bread

Ingredients

- *2 teaspoons instant yeast*
- *240 g Light Flour Blend*
- *125 g gluten-free oat flour*
- *48 g granulated cane sugar*
- *1 tablespoon baking powder*
- *1 teaspoon xanthan gum*
- *1 teaspoon kosher or fine sea salt*
- *1/8 teaspoon ascorbic acid (optional)*
- *100 g fresh cranberries*
- *60 g toasted chopped walnuts*
- *3 large eggs, at room temperature, beaten*
- *255 ml water or seltzer water, warmed to about 80°F (27°C)*
- *60 ml olive oil*
- *2 teaspoons apple cider vinegar*
- *Topping:*
- *1 tablespoon water*
- *Gluten-free oats*

Instructions

1. All ingredients should be at room temperature, 70 – 80 F.
2. Set up the bread pan and beater paddle(s). Add wet ingredients first, followed by dry ingredients into the pan.
3. Whisk the yeast in a small bowl and set it aside. In a large mixing bowl, combine all dry ingredients except cranberries and walnuts. Add cranberries and walnuts, toss, and set aside.

4. In a glass measuring cup, whisk together the wet ingredients and pour them into the bread pan. Spread the dry ingredients over the wet ones in the bread pan, ensuring coverage. Create a shallow well in the center and pour in the yeast.

5. Place the bread pan in the machine, ensuring it's settled in the center and locked in place. Choose the Gluten-free cycle, Loaf size: 1 1/2 pounds/750 g, and Medium crust setting. Start the cycle.

6. After a few minutes of mixing, check and scrape down the sides if needed. Adjust the dough consistency if it appears too wet or dry.

7. Once the mix/knead cycle finishes, gently brush the top of the dough with water and sprinkle oats on top. Avoid opening the machine during the rise and bake cycles.

8. When the bake cycle completes and the bread reaches 207°F to 210°F (97°C to 99°C) internally, remove the pan and let it cool on a wire rack. Turn the pan upside down to release the loaf and let it cool sideways for at least 2 hours before slicing.

9. Store the bread in a resealable plastic bag or airtight container on the counter for up to 3 days. For longer storage, slice and tightly wrap individual slices in plastic, place them in a resealable plastic bag, and freeze them for up to 3 months.

Cheesy Herbed Pizza

Ingredients

- *1 tablespoon instant yeast*
- *360 g Light Flour Blend or Whole-Grain Flour Blend*
- *64 g cornstarch, potato starch, or arrowroot*
- *22 g milk powder*
- *21 g cheddar cheese powder*
- *25 g finely grated Parmesan cheese*
- *1 tablespoon psyllium husk flakes or powder*
- *2 teaspoons granulated cane sugar*
- *2 teaspoons baking powder*
- *1 1/2 teaspoons kosher or fine sea salt*
- *1/2 teaspoon dried oregano*
- *1/2 teaspoon onion powder*

- *1/2 teaspoon garlic powder*
- *1/8 teaspoon ascorbic acid (optional)*
- *360 ml water, warmed to about 80°F (27°C)*
- *1 teaspoon apple cider vinegar*

Topping:

- *Pizza Sauce, pesto, shredded cheese, chopped vegetables, fresh herbs, thinly sliced meats*
- *Chopped fresh basil (optional)*

Instructions

1. All ingredients should be at room temperature, 70 – 80 F.
2. Set up the bread pan and beater paddle(s). Add wet ingredients first, followed by dry ingredients into the pan.
3. Preheat the oven to 400°F (200°C) with oven racks in the upper and lower thirds. Line and lightly oil two baking sheets with parchment paper.
4. Whisk the yeast separately. In a large mixing bowl, combine all dry ingredients except the yeast.
5. Pour the wet ingredients into the bread pan. Spread the dry ingredients over the wet ones and create a shallow well in the center for the yeast.
6. Start the Dough cycle in the bread machine. Occasionally scrape down the sides with a spatula during mixing.
7. After about 5 minutes when the dough is smooth, cancel the cycle, turn off the machine, and remove the bread pan.
8. Scoop the dough onto the prepared baking sheets, divide it into two, and shape each piece into a 10- to 12-inch rectangle. Create a shallow "moat" around the edge and dock the center with a fork.
9. Let the dough rest uncovered until it slightly rises, about 30 to 45 minutes.
10. Bake the crusts until partially cooked, 15 to 20 minutes, then add desired toppings sparingly.
11. Return pizzas to the oven, reduce heat to 350°F (180°C), and bake until golden brown and toppings are cooked, 15 to 20 minutes.

12. Transfer pizzas to wire racks using parchment, sprinkle fresh basil if desired, and let them rest for at least 5 minutes before cutting and serving.

Note: Whisk cheddar cheese powder before measuring to prevent clumping.

Apple Bacon Quinoa Bread

Ingredients

- *21 g instant yeast*
- *240 g Light Flour Blend*
- *104 g quinoa flakes*
- *44 g Better Than Milk Soy powder*
- *133 g granulated cane sugar*
- *1 tablespoon baking powder*
- *1 tablespoon psyllium husk flakes or powder*
- *2 teaspoons kosher salt*
- *1/8 teaspoon ascorbic acid (optional)*
- *6 slices bacon, cooked and crumbled*
- *3 large eggs, beaten*
- *180 ml water, heated to about 80°F (27°C)*
- *60 ml vegetable oil*
- *2 teaspoons apple cider vinegar*
- *220 g finely grated peeled apple*

Instructions

1. All ingredients should be at room temperature, 70 – 80 F.
2. Set up the bread pan and insert the beater paddle(s) in your bread machine. Add wet ingredients (except apples) into the bread pan, followed by the dry ingredients. Lastly, add the yeast.
3. In a separate mixing bowl, whisk together the dry ingredients (except bacon).
4. Stir the finely grated apples into the wet ingredient mixture in the bread pan. Then, spread the dry ingredients over the wet ingredients, ensuring coverage. Create a shallow well in the center for the yeast.

5. Place the bread pan in the machine, lock it, and select the Gluten-free cycle, a loaf size of 1 1/2 pounds/750 g, and a Medium crust. Start the cycle.

6. Around 3 minutes into the mixing, open the lid and scrape down the sides of the pan, ensuring proper mixing. Check the dough consistency during kneading, adjusting with flour blend or warm water if needed. Allow the machine to complete the kneading and rising cycles.

7. Once the bake cycle finishes, check the bread's internal temperature, aiming for 97°C to 99°C (97°C to 99°C) with an instant-read thermometer. If done, remove the bread pan from the machine and place it on a wire rack. Let it cool for a couple of minutes.

8. Turn the bread pan upside down to slide the loaf onto the wire rack. Remove the paddle if embedded. Let the bread cool upside down for at least 2 hours before slicing.

9. Store the bread in an airtight container or resealable plastic bag at room temperature for up to 3 days. For longer storage, slice, wrap tightly in plastic, and freeze for up to 3 months.

Apricot-Walnut Quick Bread

Ingredients

- 270 g Light Flour Blend
- 200 g granulated cane sugar
- 90 g millet flour
- 1 tablespoon baking powder
- 2 teaspoons psyllium husk flakes or powder
- 1 teaspoon ground ginger
- 1/2 teaspoon kosher or fine sea salt
- 1/4 cup vegetable oil or melted nondairy butter substitute (60 ml or 55 g)
- 120 ml apricot nectar or water
- 3 large eggs, beaten
- 130 g chopped dried apricots
- 60 g chopped walnuts, toasted

Instructions

1. All ingredients should be at room temperature, 70 – 80 F.

2. Set up the bread pan and beater paddle(s). Add wet ingredients first, followed by dry ingredients into the pan.

3. In a separate large mixing bowl, whisk together all the dry ingredients.

4. Combine the oil (or melted butter substitute), apricot nectar (or water), beaten eggs, chopped apricots, and toasted walnuts in a large bowl. Mix well, then transfer this mixture to the bread pan. Spread the dry ingredients evenly over the wet mixture using a spatula.

5. Set the bread machine to the Express bake cycle, a loaf size of 1 1/2 pounds/750 g, and a Light crust. Start the cycle.

6. During the first kneading cycle, ensure all the dry ingredients are well incorporated by scraping the sides and bottom of the pan with a spatula. Once mixing/kneading is complete, allow the bread machine to finish the rise and bake cycles with the lid closed.

7. Once the bake cycle finishes, check the bread's internal temperature with an instant-read thermometer. Aim for 97°C to 99°C (97°C to 99°C) for doneness. Remove the pan from the machine and cool the bread in the pan for 3 minutes. Then, carefully remove the loaf from the pan and let it cool upside down on a wire rack for at least 2 hours before slicing.

8. Store the bread in an airtight container or resealable plastic bag on the counter for up to 1 day. For longer storage, slice the bread, wrap the slices tightly in plastic wrap, place them in a resealable plastic bag, and freeze for up to 3 months.

Banana Quick Bread Recipe

Ingredients

- 240 g Light Flour Blend
- 200 g granulated cane sugar
- 60 g millet flour
- 23 g unsweetened cocoa powder
- 1 tablespoon baking powder
- 1 tablespoon psyllium husk flakes or powder
- 2 teaspoons instant espresso powder
- 1/2 teaspoon kosher or fine sea salt
- 3 large ripe bananas
- 1/3 cup vegetable oil or melted nondairy butter substitute (80 ml or 75 g/2.6 oz)

- 3 large eggs, beaten

Instructions

1. All ingredients should be at room temperature, 70 – 80 F.

2. Set up the bread pan and beater paddle(s). Add wet ingredients first, followed by dry ingredients into the pan.

3. In a separate large mixing bowl, whisk together all the dry ingredients.

4. Mash the bananas into a paste in a large bowl using a fork or potato masher. Add the oil and beaten eggs, whisk until smooth, then pour this mixture into the bread pan. Spread the dry ingredients evenly over the wet mixture using a spatula.

5. Set the bread machine to the Express bake cycle, a loaf size of 1 1/2 pounds/750 g, and a Light crust. Start the cycle.

6. During the first kneading cycle, ensure all the dry ingredients are well incorporated by scraping the sides and bottom of the pan with a spatula. Once mixing/kneading is complete, allow the bread machine to finish the rise and bake cycles with the lid closed.

7. Once the bake cycle finishes, check the bread's internal temperature with an instant-read thermometer. Aim for 97°C to 99°C (97°C to 99°C) for doneness. Remove the pan from the machine and cool the bread in the pan for 3 minutes. Then, carefully remove the loaf from the pan and let it cool upside down on a wire rack for at least 2 hours before slicing.

8. Store the bread in an airtight container or resealable plastic bag on the counter for up to 3 days. For longer storage, slice the bread, wrap the slices tightly in plastic wrap, place them in a resealable plastic bag, and freeze for up to 3 months.

Blueberry Quick Bread Recipe

Ingredients

- *180g Light Flour Blend or Whole-Grain Flour Blend*
- *120g millet flour*
- *200g granulated cane sugar*
- *1 tablespoon baking powder*
- *2 teaspoons psyllium husk flakes or powder*
- *1 teaspoon kosher or fine sea salt*

- *120 ml unsweetened coconut milk, warmed to about 80°F (27°C)*
- *80 ml vegetable oil*
- *3 large eggs, at room temperature, beaten*
- *1 teaspoon pure vanilla extract*
- *180g fresh blueberries, rinsed and patted dry*

Topping:

- *75g brown sugar*
- *2 tablespoons Light Flour Blend or Whole-Grain Flour Blend*
- *1/8 teaspoon ground cinnamon, nutmeg, mace, or cardamom*

Instructions

1. All ingredients should be at room temperature, 70 – 80 F.
2. Set up the bread pan and beater paddle(s). Add wet ingredients first, followed by dry ingredients into the pan.
3. Whisk together the dry ingredients in a large mixing bowl.
4. In a separate 4-cup glass measuring cup, whisk the wet ingredients together, then pour this mixture into the bread pan. Use a spatula to evenly spread the dry ingredients over the wet mixture.
5. Set the bread machine to the Quick bread/cake cycle, a loaf size of 1 1/2 pounds/750 g, and a Light crust. Start the cycle.
6. During the first knead cycle, scrape the sides and bottom of the pan to ensure all dry ingredients are fully mixed. Add the blueberries and allow the machine to continue kneading.
7. In a small bowl, mix the topping ingredients using a fork.
8. When the machine signals the transition from kneading to baking, remove the paddle, reshape the loaf if needed, and sprinkle the prepared topping evenly over the dough.
9. Allow the bread to finish baking. Check the bread's internal temperature with an instant-read thermometer. It should register between 97°C to 99°C (97°C to 99°C) when done.
10. Once baked, remove the pan from the machine and cool the bread in the pan for 3 minutes. Then, slide the loaf out of the pan onto a wire rack, allowing it to cool on its side for at least an hour before slicing.

11. Store the cooled bread in a resealable plastic bag or an airtight container on the counter for up to 3 days. For longer storage, slice the bread, tightly wrap the slices in plastic, place them in a resealable plastic bag, and freeze for up to 3 months.

Caramel Apple Quick Bread

Ingredients

- *300 g Light Flour Blend*
- *200 g granulated cane sugar*
- *65 g teff flour*
- *44 g Better Than Milk Soy powder*
- *1 tablespoon baking powder*
- *1 tablespoon psyllium husk flakes or powder*
- *1 teaspoon kosher or fine sea salt*
- *3 large eggs, at room temperature, beaten*
- *120 ml applesauce*
- *80 ml vegetable oil*
- *220 g grated peeled apples*
- *312 g gluten-free caramel bits or quartered standard caramel squares*

Instructions

1. All ingredients should be at room temperature, 70 – 80 F.
2. Set up the bread pan and beater paddle(s). Add wet ingredients first, followed by dry ingredients into the pan.
3. Whisk together the dry ingredients in a large mixing bowl.
4. In another large mixing bowl, whisk together the beaten eggs, applesauce, and vegetable oil. Add the grated apples and caramel bits, then scrape this mixture into the bread pan. Use a spatula to spread the dry ingredients evenly over the wet mixture.
5. Set the bread machine to the Quick bread/cake cycle, a loaf size of 1 1/2 pounds/750 g, and a Medium crust. Start the cycle.

6. About 3 minutes into the mixing process, open the lid and scrape down the sides of the pan, ensuring any accumulated flour is incorporated into the dough. Check the dough's consistency during kneading and adjust with small amounts of flour blend or warm water if needed.

7. When the bake cycle completes, check the bread's internal temperature with an instant-read thermometer. It should read between 97°C to 99°C (97°C to 99°C).

8. Remove the bread pan from the machine and place it on a wire cooling rack. Allow the bread to rest in the pan for a few minutes, then carefully remove the loaf from the pan and let it cool upside down for at least 2 hours before slicing.

9. Store the cooled bread in a resealable plastic bag or airtight container on the counter for up to 3 days. For longer storage, slice the bread, tightly wrap the slices in plastic, place them in a resealable plastic bag, and freeze for up to 3 months.

Fruitcake Recipe

Ingredients

Fruit Mixture

- *455 g dried fruit, diced*
- *210 g candied cherries, chopped*
- *80 ml brandy, rum, or whiskey*
- *1 tablespoon pure vanilla extract*
- *21 g instant yeast*
- *240 g Light Flour Blend or Whole-Grain Flour Blend*
- *133 g granulated cane sugar*
- *1 tablespoon baking powder*
- *1 tablespoon psyllium husk flakes or powder*
- *1 teaspoon ground nutmeg*
- *3/4 teaspoon ground cinnamon*
- *3/4 teaspoon kosher or fine sea salt*
- *112 g non-dairy butter substitute, melted*
- *85 g molasses*
- *3 large eggs, beaten*

- *2 teaspoons orange extract*
- *56 g chopped pecans or other nuts*

Instructions

1. All ingredients should be at room temperature, 70 – 80 F.
2. Microwave the dried fruit mixture with alcohol and vanilla for 5 minutes, then set it aside to macerate.
3. Set up the bread pan and beater paddle(s). Add wet ingredients first, followed by dry ingredients into the pan.
4. Combine the yeast with a small portion in a bowl and set it aside. Whisk the remaining dry ingredients in a large bowl.
5. Whisk the wet ingredients together in a glass measuring cup, then pour them into the bread pan. Spread the dry ingredients evenly over the wet mixture and create a shallow well to add the yeast. Put the bread pan in the machine, set it for a Gluten-free cycle, 1 1/2 pounds/750 g loaf size, and Medium crust. Initiate the cycle.
6. After the first kneading cycle, scrape the pan's sides to integrate any dry ingredients. Add the macerated fruit mixture and nuts when the machine prompts. Keep the lid closed for the remainder of the rise and bake cycles.
7. When the bake cycle ends, check the loaf's temperature with an instant-read thermometer (97°C to 99°C). Remove the pan from the machine, place it on a wire rack, and let the bread rest in the pan before sliding it onto the rack. Allow it to cool on its side for 2 hours.
8. Store the fruitcake in an airtight container or resealable plastic bag at room temperature for up to 2 weeks. For extended storage, slice and tightly wrap in plastic, then freeze in a resealable plastic bag for up to 3 months.

Lemon Quick Bread

Ingredients

- *300 g Light Flour Blend*
- *56 g almond flour/meal*
- *1/2 cup Better Than Milk soy powder or coconut milk powder (40-44 g)*
- *250 g granulated cane sugar*

- *1 tablespoon baking powder*
- *1 tablespoon psyllium husk flakes or powder*
- *1 teaspoon kosher or fine sea salt*
- *3 large eggs, beaten*
- *Grated zest of 1 lemon*
- *120 ml freshly squeezed lemon juice*
- *80 ml vegetable or canola oil*

Instructions

1. All ingredients should be at room temperature, 70 – 80 F.
2. Set up the bread pan and beater paddle(s). Add wet ingredients first, followed by dry ingredients into the pan.
3. Whisk together the dry ingredients in a large mixing bowl.
4. Combine the wet ingredients in a glass measuring cup, then pour them into the bread pan. Ensure the dry ingredients cover the wet mixture entirely.
5. Place the bread pan in the machine, settle it properly, and lock it in place. Choose the Quick bread/cake cycle, 1 1/2 pounds/750 g loaf size, and Medium crust setting. Initiate the cycle.
6. About 3 minutes into mixing, open the lid and scrape down the sides of the pan with a spatula, ensuring even mixing. Adjust the dough consistency if needed by adding small amounts of flour blend or water.
7. Once the bake cycle finishes, check the internal temperature of the bread (97°C to 99°C). Remove the pan, set it on a wire rack, and allow the bread to cool upside down for a few minutes. Then, gently remove the loaf from the pan and let it cool upside down for at least 2 hours before slicing.
8. Store the cooled bread in an airtight container or resealable plastic bag on the counter for up to 3 days. For longer storage, slice and tightly wrap individual slices in plastic, place them in a resealable plastic bag, and freeze them for up to 3 months.

Lime-Poppy Seed Quick Bread

Ingredients

- *300 g Light Flour Blend*

- *60 g millet flour*

- *44 g Better Than Milk Soy powder*

- *200 g granulated cane sugar*

- *2 tablespoons poppy seeds*

- *1 tablespoon baking powder*

- *1 tablespoon psyllium husk flakes or powder*

- *1 teaspoon kosher or fine sea salt*

- *3 large eggs, beaten*

- *120 ml water, heated to about 80°F (27°C)*

- *Grated zest of 1 lime*

- *90 ml freshly squeezed lime juice*

- *60 ml vegetable or canola oil*

Instructions

1. All ingredients should be at room temperature, 70 – 80 F.

2. Set up the bread pan and beater paddle(s). Add wet ingredients first, followed by dry ingredients into the pan.

3. Whisk the dry ingredients together in a large mixing bowl.

4. Combine the wet ingredients in a glass measuring cup, then pour them into the bread pan. Ensure the dry ingredients cover the wet mixture completely.

5. Place the bread pan in the machine, ensuring it's centered and locked. Choose the Quick bread/cake cycle, 1 1/2 pounds/750 g loaf size, and Medium crust setting. Start the cycle.

6. Around 3 minutes into the mixing, open the lid and scrape down the pan's sides with a spatula, avoiding the paddle. Adjust the dough consistency if needed by adding small amounts of flour blend or water.

7. Once the bake cycle completes, check the bread's internal temperature (97°C to 99°C). Remove the pan from the machine, place it on a wire rack on its side, and let it sit for a few minutes. Then, invert the pan and gently slide the loaf onto the wire rack. Carefully remove the paddle if it's attached. Allow the bread to cool upside down for at least 2 hours before slicing.

8. Store the cooled bread in an airtight container or resealable plastic bag on the counter for up to 3 days. For longer storage, slice the bread, wrap each slice tightly in plastic, place them in a resealable plastic bag, and freeze for up to 3 months.

Nut 'n' Fruit Bread

Ingredients

- 240 g Light Flour Blend or Whole-Grain Flour Blend
- 2 teaspoons instant yeast
- 1 tablespoon psyllium husk flakes or powder
- 1/2 teaspoon kosher or fine sea salt
- 145 g golden raisins
- 145 g dark raisins or currants
- 145 g chopped dates
- 145 g quartered dried apricots
- 55 g chopped pecans
- 55 g chopped walnuts
- 55 g sliced almonds
- 400 ml unsweetened coconut milk, warmed to about 80°F (27°C)

Instructions

1. All ingredients should be at room temperature, 70 – 80 F.
2. Set up the bread pan and beater paddle(s). Add wet ingredients first, followed by dry ingredients into the pan.
3. In a large mixing bowl, combine the flour blend, yeast, psyllium, and salt. Add the dried fruits and nuts. Mix well to coat the fruits and nuts evenly with the dry ingredients.
4. Pour the warmed coconut milk into the bread pan. Add the dry ingredients to the pan, ensuring they cover the milk entirely.
5. Place the bread pan in the machine, ensuring it's centered and locked. Select the Quick bread/cake cycle, 1 1/2 pounds/750 g loaf size, and Medium crust setting. Start the cycle.
6. After the first kneading cycle, scrape the sides and bottom of the pan with a spatula to ensure all dry ingredients are incorporated. The dough might appear dry, which is normal for this

dense bread. After the second kneading cycle, remove the paddle and smooth the top of the dough. Avoid opening the lid during the bake cycle.

7. Once the bake cycle finishes, check the bread's internal temperature (97°C to 99°C). Remove the pan from the machine, place it on a wire rack on its side, and let it sit for 3 minutes. Then, invert the pan and gently slide the loaf onto the wire rack. Allow the bread to cool on its side for at least 2 hours before slicing.

8. Store the cooled bread in an airtight container or resealable plastic bag on the counter for up to 3 days. For longer storage, slice the bread, double-wrap each slice tightly in plastic, place them in a resealable plastic bag, and freeze for up to 3 months.

Orange-Glazed Quick Bread

Ingredients

- 300 g Light Flour Blend or Whole-Grain Flour Blend
- 200 g granulated cane sugar
- 60 g millet flour
- 20 g coconut milk powder
- 1 tablespoon baking powder
- 1 tablespoon psyllium husk flakes or powder
- 1 teaspoon kosher or fine sea salt
- 80 ml vegetable oil
- 3 large eggs, at room temperature, beaten
- 120 ml freshly squeezed orange juice or water, warmed to about 80°F (27°C)
- 1 teaspoon orange extract
- 44 g finely chopped candied orange peel
- Glaze:
- 90 g confectioners' sugar
- 30 ml freshly squeezed orange juice
- 15 to 30 ml hot water, as needed

Instructions

1. All ingredients should be at room temperature, 70 – 80 F.

2. Set up the bread pan and beater paddle(s). Add wet ingredients first, followed by dry ingredients into the pan.

3. In a large mixing bowl, whisk together the dry ingredients.

4. In a separate bowl or measuring cup, combine the wet ingredients (except the candied orange peel). Stir in the candied orange peel and pour this mixture into the bread pan. Spread the dry ingredients over the wet mixture using a spatula.

5. Place the bread pan in the machine and ensure it's properly settled. Select the Quick bread/cake cycle, 1 1/2 pounds/750 g loaf size, and Medium crust setting. Start the cycle.

6. After the first kneading cycle, use a spatula to scrape down the sides and bottom of the pan to ensure all the dry ingredients are incorporated.

7. When the machine signals the transition from knead to bake cycle, remove the kneading paddle and reshape the loaf if necessary. If the dough seems sticky, wet your hands slightly to smooth the top of the loaf. Let the bread finish baking without opening the lid.

8. Once the bake cycle is complete, check the internal temperature of the bread (97°C to 99°C). Remove the pan from the machine and place it on a wire rack. After a couple of minutes, invert the pan to slide the loaf onto the wire rack. Let it cool on its side for at least 2 hours before glazing.

9. For the glaze, whisk together the confectioners' sugar and orange juice in a small bowl. Add hot water gradually until the desired consistency is achieved. Drizzle the glaze over the cooled bread and allow it to set for around 15 minutes before slicing.

10. Store the glazed bread in a resealable plastic bag or airtight container at room temperature for up to 3 days. For longer storage, slice and wrap the slices tightly in plastic, then place them in a resealable plastic bag and freeze for up to 3 months.

Pear-Ginger Quick Bread

Ingredients

- *360 g Light Flour Blend*
- *44 g Better Than Milk Soy powder*
- *200 g granulated cane sugar*
- *1 tablespoon psyllium husk flakes or powder*
- *2 teaspoons baking powder*

- *1 teaspoon kosher or fine sea salt*
- *3 large eggs, at room temperature, beaten*
- *180 ml water, warmed to about 80°F (27°C)*
- *60 ml vegetable or canola oil*
- *2 teaspoons pure vanilla extract*
- *2 teaspoons grated peeled fresh ginger*
- *Add-Ins:*
- *220 g grated peeled Bosc pear*
- *118 g finely chopped crystallized or candied ginger*

Instructions

1. All ingredients should be at room temperature, 70 – 80 F.
2. Set up the bread pan and beater paddle(s). Add wet ingredients first, followed by dry ingredients into the pan.
3. In a large mixing bowl, whisk together the dry ingredients.
4. In a separate bowl or measuring cup, combine the wet ingredients (excluding the pear and crystallized ginger). Pour this mixture into the bread pan. Spread the dry ingredients over the wet mixture using a spatula.
5. Place the bread pan in the machine and ensure it's properly settled. Select the Quick bread/cake cycle, 1 1/2 pounds/750 g loaf size, and Medium crust setting. Start the cycle.
6. About 3 minutes into the mixing process, open the lid and use a spatula to scrape down the sides of the pan to ensure all ingredients are mixed well.
7. After the first kneading cycle, add the grated pear and crystallized ginger. Let the machine finish its cycle without opening the lid.
8. When the baking cycle completes, check the bread's internal temperature (97°C to 99°C). Remove the pan from the machine and place it on a wire rack. After a couple of minutes, invert the pan to slide the loaf onto the wire rack. Let it cool on its side for at least 2 hours before slicing.
9. Store the bread in a resealable plastic bag or airtight container at room temperature for up to 3 days. For longer storage, slice and wrap the slices tightly in plastic, then place them in a resealable plastic bag and freeze for up to 3 months.

Pineapple-Coconut Quick Bread

Ingredients

- *300 g Light Flour Blend*
- *59 g coconut flour*
- *200 g granulated cane sugar*
- *1 tablespoon psyllium husk flakes or powder*
- *2 teaspoons baking powder*
- *1 teaspoon kosher or fine sea salt*
- *3 large eggs, at room temperature, beaten*
- *240 ml unsweetened coconut milk, warmed to about 80°F (27°C)*
- *80 ml vegetable or canola oil*
- *2 teaspoons pure vanilla extract*
- *Add-Ins:*
- *170 g sweetened shredded coconut*
- *168 g chopped dried pineapple*

Instructions

1. All ingredients should be at room temperature, 70 – 80 F.
2. Set up the bread pan and beater paddle(s). Add wet ingredients first, followed by dry ingredients into the pan.
3. In a large mixing bowl, whisk together the dry ingredients.
4. In a separate bowl or measuring cup, combine the wet ingredients (except the add-ins: shredded coconut and dried pineapple). Pour this mixture into the bread pan. Spread the dry ingredients over the wet mixture using a spatula.
5. Place the bread pan in the machine and ensure it's properly settled. Select the Quick bread/cake cycle, 1 1/2 pounds/750 g loaf size, and Medium crust setting. Start the cycle.
6. About 3 minutes into the mixing process, open the lid and use a spatula to scrape down the sides of the pan to ensure all ingredients are mixed well.
7. After the first knead cycle, add the shredded coconut and chopped dried pineapple. Let the machine finish its cycle without opening the lid.

8. When the baking cycle completes, check the bread's internal temperature (97°C to 99°C). Remove the pan from the machine and place it on a wire rack. After a couple of minutes, invert the pan to slide the loaf onto the wire rack. Let it cool on its side for at least 2 hours before slicing.

9. Store the bread in a resealable plastic bag or airtight container at room temperature for up to 3 days. For longer storage, slice and wrap the slices tightly in plastic, then place them in a resealable plastic bag and freeze for up to 3 months.

Trail Mix Bread

Ingredients

- *21 g instant yeast*
- *360 g Light Flour Blend*
- *44 g Better Than Milk Soy powder*
- *100 g granulated cane sugar*
- *1 tablespoon psyllium husk flakes or powder*
- *2 teaspoons baking powder*
- *1 teaspoon kosher or fine sea salt*
- *1/8 teaspoon ascorbic acid (optional)*
- *3 large eggs, at room temperature, beaten*
- *240 ml water, heated to about 80°F (27°C)*
- *60 ml vegetable or canola oil*
- *2 teaspoons ume plum vinegar*
- *2 teaspoons pure vanilla extract*
  Add-In:
- *300 g gluten-free, dairy-free trail mix*

Instructions

1. All ingredients should be at room temperature, 70 – 80 F.
2. Set up the bread pan and beater paddle(s). Add wet ingredients first, followed by dry ingredients into the pan.

3. Measure the yeast into a small bowl and set it aside. In a large mixing bowl, whisk together the remaining dry ingredients.

4. In a separate bowl or measuring cup, whisk the wet ingredients together (except the yeast). Pour this mixture into the bread pan. Spread the dry ingredients over the wet mixture using a spatula. Create a shallow well in the center and add the yeast.

5. Place the bread pan in the machine and ensure it's properly settled. Choose the Gluten-free cycle, 1 1/2 pounds/750 g loaf size, and Medium crust setting. Start the cycle.

6. Around 3 minutes into the mixing process, open the lid and use a spatula to scrape down the sides of the pan to ensure all ingredients are well mixed.

7. After the initial kneading cycle, add the trail mix to the dough. Let the machine finish the cycle without opening the lid.

8. When the baking cycle finishes, check the bread's internal temperature (97°C to 99°C). Remove the pan from the machine and place it on a wire rack. After a few minutes, invert the pan to slide the loaf onto the wire rack. Let it cool upside down for at least 2 hours before slicing.

9. Store the bread in a resealable plastic bag or airtight container at room temperature for up to 3 days. For longer storage, slice and wrap the slices tightly in plastic, then place them in a resealable plastic bag and freeze for up to 3 months.

Zucchini-Applesauce Quick Bread

Ingredients

- 180 g Light Flour Blend or Whole-Grain Flour Blend
- 118 g millet flour
- 250 g granulated cane sugar
- 2 teaspoons baking powder
- 2 teaspoons psyllium husk flakes or powder
- 1 teaspoon kosher or fine sea salt
- 3/4 teaspoon ground cinnamon
- 3 large eggs, at room temperature, beaten
- 125 g applesauce
- 80 ml vegetable oil

- 2 teaspoons pure vanilla extract
- 120 g grated peeled zucchini

  Add-In:

- 85 g gluten-free, dairy-free semisweet chocolate chips

Instructions

1. All ingredients should be at room temperature, 70 – 80 F.
2. Set up the bread pan and beater paddle(s). Add wet ingredients first, followed by dry ingredients into the pan.
3. In a large mixing bowl, whisk together the dry ingredients.
4. In another bowl or measuring cup, whisk the wet ingredients (except the zucchini). Stir in the grated zucchini and pour this mixture into the bread pan. Use a spatula to spread the dry ingredients over the wet ingredients.
5. Place the bread pan in the machine, ensuring it's centered and locked. Choose the Quick bread/cake cycle, 1 1/2 pounds/750 g loaf size, and Medium crust setting. Start the cycle.
6. After the initial kneading cycle, when there's an opportunity to add ingredients (if your machine allows), add the chocolate chips to the batter. If not, add them once the mixing/kneading is complete, before the baking cycle.
7. Allow the machine to complete the baking cycle. Check the bread's internal temperature (97°C to 99°C) to ensure it's done.
8. When baking is finished, remove the pan and place it on a wire rack. After a couple of minutes, invert the pan to release the loaf onto the rack. Allow the bread to cool on its side for at least 2 hours before slicing.
9. Store the bread in a resealable plastic bag or airtight container at room temperature for up to 3 days. For longer storage, slice and wrap individual slices tightly in plastic, then place them in a resealable plastic bag, and freeze them for up to 3 months.

Butternut Squash Quick Bread

Ingredients

- *300 g Light Flour Blend or Whole-Grain Flour Blend*
- *56 g butternut squash flour*

- *100 g granulated cane sugar*
- *1 tablespoon baking powder*
- *1 tablespoon psyllium husk flakes or powder*
- *1 teaspoon kosher or fine sea salt*
- *3/4 teaspoon ground nutmeg*
- *3 large eggs, at room temperature, beaten*
- *120 ml unsweetened coconut milk*
- *60 ml vegetable oil*
- *2 teaspoons pure vanilla extract*
- *140 g grated peeled butternut squash*

Instructions

1. All ingredients should be at room temperature, 70 – 80 F.
2. Set up the bread pan and beater paddle(s). Add wet ingredients first, followed by dry ingredients into the pan.
3. In a large mixing bowl, whisk together the dry ingredients.
4. In another bowl or measuring cup, whisk the wet ingredients (except the grated squash). Stir in the grated squash and pour this mixture into the bread pan. Use a spatula to spread the dry ingredients over the wet ingredients.
5. Place the bread pan in the machine, ensuring it's centered and locked. Choose the Quick bread/cake cycle, 1 1/2 pounds/750 g loaf size, and Light crust setting. Start the cycle.
6. After the initial kneading cycle, if your machine allows, remove the paddle and reshape the loaf. If the dough seems sticky, wet your hands slightly to reshape the loaf and smooth the top. Allow the bread to finish baking undisturbed.
7. Once the baking cycle is complete, check the bread's internal temperature (97°C to 99°C) using an instant-read thermometer inserted into the center.
8. After baking, remove the pan from the machine and let it sit on its side on a wire rack for 3 minutes. Then, gently slide the loaf out of the pan and allow it to cool on its side for at least 1 hour before slicing.

9. Store the bread in a resealable plastic bag or airtight container at room temperature for up to 3 days. For longer storage, slice and double wrap individual slices tightly in plastic, then place in a resealable plastic bag, and freeze for up to 3 months.

Carrot-Raisin Bread

Ingredients

- *2 teaspoons instant yeast*
- *360 g Light Flour Blend*
- *44 g Better Than Milk Soy powder*
- *100 g granulated cane sugar*
- *2 tablespoons baking powder*
- *1 tablespoon psyllium husk flakes or powder*
- *1 teaspoon kosher or fine sea salt*
- *1/8 teaspoon ascorbic acid (optional)*
- *3 large eggs*
- *180 ml carrot juice, warmed to about 80°F (27°C)*
- *60 ml vegetable or canola oil*
- *2 teaspoons ume plum vinegar*
- *180 g shredded peeled carrots*
- *145 g golden raisins*

Instructions

1. All ingredients should be at room temperature, 70 – 80 F.
2. Set up the bread pan and beater paddle(s). Add wet ingredients first, followed by dry ingredients into the pan.
3. Measure the yeast into a small bowl and set it aside. In a large mixing bowl, whisk together the remaining dry ingredients.
4. In a separate bowl or measuring cup, whisk the wet ingredients (except carrots and raisins) together. Stir in the shredded carrots and raisins, then pour this mixture into the bread pan. Use a spatula to spread the dry ingredients over the wet ingredients.

5. Place the bread pan in the machine, ensuring it's centered and locked. Select the Gluten-free cycle, 1 1/2 pounds/750 g loaf size, and Medium crust setting. Start the cycle.

6. About 3 minutes into the mixing process, open the lid and use a spatula to scrape down the sides of the pan, avoiding the paddle. Check the dough consistency during kneading, adjusting with flour blend or warm water if needed.

7. After the baking cycle completes, check the bread's internal temperature (97°C to 99°C) using an instant-read thermometer inserted into the center.

8. Once baked, remove the pan from the machine and let it sit on its side on a wire rack for a couple of minutes. Then, gently slide the loaf out of the pan and allow it to cool upside down for at least 2 hours before slicing.

9. Store the bread in a resealable plastic bag or airtight container at room temperature for up to 3 days. For longer storage, slice the bread, wrap individual slices tightly in plastic, place in a resealable plastic bag, and freeze for up to 3 months.

Chocolate-Peanut Butter Quick Bread

Ingredients

- *300 g Light Flour Blend or Whole-Grain Flour Blend*
- *200 g granulated cane sugar*
- *55 g sweet ground chocolate*
- *24 g powdered peanut butter*
- *40 g DariFree*
- *1 tablespoon baking powder*
- *1 teaspoon xanthan gum*
- *3/4 teaspoon salt*
- *Wet Ingredients:*
- *1/3 cup vegetable oil or melted nondairy butter substitute (slightly cooled)*
- *3 large eggs, beaten*
- *180 ml chocolate coconut or hemp milk*
- *2 teaspoons apple cider vinegar*
  Add-In:
- *255 g peanut butter chips (optional)*

Instructions

1. All ingredients should be at room temperature, 70 – 80 F.

2. Set up the bread pan and beater paddle(s). Add wet ingredients first, followed by dry ingredients into the pan.

3. Whisk the dry ingredients together in a large mixing bowl.

4. Combine the wet ingredients in a glass measuring cup and pour them into the bread pan. Use a spatula to cover the wet ingredients with the dry mixture completely.

5. Place the bread pan in the machine, ensuring it's centered and locked. Select the Quick bread/cake cycle, 1 1/2 pounds/750 g loaf size, and Medium crust setting. Start the cycle.

6. After the initial kneading cycle, scrape down the sides and bottom of the pan to ensure all dry ingredients are incorporated. Add the peanut butter chips if desired. Let the machine continue the kneading, rising, and baking.

7. Once the baking cycle finishes, check the bread's internal temperature (97°C to 99°C) with an instant-read thermometer inserted into the center.

8. Remove the pan from the machine and let it rest on a wire rack for a couple of minutes. Then, gently slide the loaf out and let it cool on its side for at least an hour before slicing.

9. Store the bread in a resealable plastic bag or airtight container at room temperature for up to 3 days. For longer storage, slice the bread, wrap individual slices tightly in plastic, place in a resealable plastic bag, and freeze for up to 3 months.

Honey Granola Bread

Ingredients

- *21 g instant yeast*
- *240 g Light Flour Blend*
- *120 g oat flour*
- *150 g granulated cane sugar*
- *44 g Better Than Milk Soy powder*
- *1 tablespoon baking powder*
- *1 tablespoon psyllium husk flakes or powder*
- *1 teaspoon kosher salt*

- *1/8 teaspoon ascorbic acid (optional)*
- *Wet Ingredients:*
- *85 g honey*
- *180 ml water (heated to about 80°F/27°C)*
- *3 large eggs, beaten*
- *60 ml vegetable or canola oil*
- *2 teaspoons apple cider vinegar*
- *2 teaspoons pure vanilla extract*
- *200 g gluten-free granola*

Instructions

1. All ingredients should be at room temperature, 70 – 80 F.
2. Set up the bread pan and beater paddle(s). Add wet ingredients first, followed by dry ingredients into the pan.
3. Whisk the dry ingredients together in a large mixing bowl.
4. In a glass measuring cup, dissolve honey in water. Add the remaining wet ingredients (except granola), whisk thoroughly, and then stir in the granola. Pour this mixture into the bread pan, ensuring the dry ingredients are fully covered. Make a shallow well in the center and add the yeast.
5. Place the bread pan in the machine, ensuring it's properly settled and locked. Choose the Gluten-free cycle, 1 1/2 pounds/750 g loaf size, and Medium crust setting. Start the cycle.
6. Check the dough during the initial mixing process, scraping down the sides to ensure all ingredients are combined. Adjust with tiny amounts of flour blend or warm water if needed. Allow the machine to complete the kneading, rising, and baking.
7. When the baking cycle finishes, check the bread's internal temperature with an instant-read thermometer (97°C to 99°C) to ensure it's done. Remove the pan from the machine and cool the bread on a wire rack, allowing it to rest upside down for at least 2 hours before slicing.
8. Store the bread in a resealable plastic bag or airtight container at room temperature for up to 3 days. For longer storage, slice and tightly wrap individual slices in plastic before freezing for up to 3 months.

Chai Latte Bread

Ingredients

- *240 g Light Flour Blend or Whole-Grain Flour Blend*
- *118 g millet flour*
- *250 g granulated cane sugar*
- *46 g dairy-free chai powder*
- *1 tablespoon baking powder*
- *2 teaspoons psyllium husk flakes or powder*
- *2 teaspoons instant espresso powder*
- *1 teaspoon kosher salt*
- *Wet Ingredients:*
- *120 ml unsweetened soy or coconut milk*
- *80 ml vegetable oil*
- *3 large eggs, beaten*
- *1 teaspoon pure vanilla extract*

Instructions

1. All ingredients should be at room temperature, 70 – 80 F.
2. Set up the bread pan and beater paddle(s). Add wet ingredients first, followed by dry ingredients into the pan.
3. Whisk the dry ingredients in a large mixing bowl.
4. Whisk the wet ingredients together in a glass measuring cup and pour them into the bread pan. Use a spatula to spread the dry ingredients over the wet mixture.
5. Set the machine to the Quick bread/cake cycle, 1 1/2 pounds/750 g loaf size, and Medium crust setting. Start the cycle.
6. After the initial kneading cycle, ensure all dry ingredients are incorporated by scraping the sides and bottom of the pan with a spatula. Let the machine complete the rest of the baking cycle without opening the lid.
7. When the bake cycle ends, use an instant-read thermometer to check if the bread registers 97°C to 99°C (97°C to 99°C) in the center. Remove the pan from the machine, place it on a wire

rack on its side for a couple of minutes, then carefully remove the loaf from the pan and let it cool on its side for at least 2 hours before slicing.

8. Store the bread in a resealable plastic bag or airtight container at room temperature for up to 3 days. For longer storage, slice the bread, tightly wrap individual slices in plastic, and freeze them for up to 3 months.

Gingerbread

Ingredients

- *2 teaspoons instant yeast*
- *360 g Light Flour Blend*
- *200 g granulated cane sugar*
- *1 tablespoon baking powder*
- *1 tablespoon psyllium husk flakes or powder*
- *16.5 g ground ginger*
- *3/4 teaspoon ground cloves*
- *1/2 teaspoon ground cinnamon*
- *1/2 teaspoon kosher salt*
- *Wet Ingredients:*
- *340 g unsulfured molasses (not blackstrap)*
- *180 ml water, heated to about 80°F (27°C)*
- *1/4 cup vegetable oil (60 ml) or melted nondairy butter substitute (55 g/2 oz or 1/2 stick)*
- *3 large eggs, beaten*

Instructions

1. All ingredients should be at room temperature, 70 – 80 F.
2. Set the bread pan and insert the beater paddle(s). Add the wet ingredients first, then add the dry ingredients.
3. Set yeast aside in a small bowl. Whisk the remaining dry ingredients together in a large mixing bowl.

4. In a glass measuring cup, dissolve molasses in warm water, then add the remaining wet ingredients. Pour into the bread pan, spreading dry ingredients over it. Make a well in the center and add the yeast.

5. Place the bread pan in the machine, select Quick bread/cake cycle, 1 1/2 pounds/750 g loaf size, and Medium crust setting. Start the cycle.

6. After the initial kneading cycle, ensure all dry ingredients are incorporated by scraping the sides and bottom of the pan. Let the machine complete the rise and bake cycles without opening the lid.

7. Once the bake cycle ends and the bread reaches 97°C to 99°C (97°C to 99°C) in the center, remove the pan and let it rest on a wire rack on its side for 3 minutes. Then, carefully remove the loaf from the pan and let it cool upside down on the wire rack for at least 2 hours before slicing.

8. Store the Gingerbread in a resealable plastic bag or airtight container at room temperature for up to 3 days. For longer storage, slice, wrap tightly, and freeze individual portions for up to 3 months.

Quick Coffee Cake Loaf

Ingredients

- *240 g Light Flour Blend or Whole-Grain Flour Blend*
- *118 g millet flour*
- *200 g granulated cane sugar*
- *1 tablespoon baking powder*
- *2 teaspoons psyllium husk flakes or powder*
- *1 teaspoon kosher or fine sea salt*
- *Wet Ingredients:*
- *125 g unsweetened applesauce*
- *1/4 cup vegetable oil (60 ml) or melted nondairy butter substitute (55 g/2 oz or 1/2 stick)*
- *3 large eggs, beaten*
- *2 teaspoons pure vanilla extract*
- *Streusel Topping:*
- *170 g light brown sugar*

- *60 g Light Flour Blend or Whole-Grain Flour Blend*
- *1/4 teaspoon kosher or fine sea salt*
- *42 g non-dairy butter substitute, chilled and cubed*

Instructions

1. All ingredients should be at room temperature, 70 – 80 F.
2. Set up the bread pan and beater paddle(s). Add wet ingredients, followed by dry ingredients, into the pan.
3. Whisk together the dry ingredients in a large mixing bowl.
4. Combine the wet ingredients in a glass measuring cup, then pour into the bread pan. Spread dry ingredients over the wet mix.
5. Place the bread pan in the machine. Select Quick bread/cake cycle - Loaf size: 1 1/2 pounds/750 g - Light crust. Start the cycle.
6. While mixing, prepare the streusel by combining its ingredients to create a wet sand-like texture.
7. After the initial kneading cycle, ensure all dry ingredients are incorporated by scraping the pan's sides and bottom.
8. During the rise cycle alert, remove the kneading paddle, reshape the loaf, and sprinkle evenly with streusel. Let the cycle complete.
9. When done, check the internal temperature (97°C to 99°C). Remove the pan and cool the loaf on a wire rack for 3 minutes. Then, invert the pan to remove the loaf and let it cool on its side for at least 2 hours before slicing.
10. Store the Gingerbread in a resealable plastic bag or airtight container at room temperature for up to 3 days. For longer storage, slice, wrap tightly, and freeze in a resealable plastic bag for up to 3 months.

Coconut Curry Quick Bread

Ingredients

- 360 g Light Flour Blend
- 150 g granulated cane sugar
- 1 tablespoon baking powder

- 1 tablespoon psyllium husk flakes or powder

- 2 teaspoons vadouvan or other curry powder

- 1 teaspoon kosher salt

- 1/8 teaspoon ascorbic acid (optional)

- Wet Ingredients:

- 3 large eggs, beaten

- 240 ml unsweetened coconut milk (heated to about 80°F/27°C)

- 60 ml vegetable or canola oil

- 2 teaspoons apple cider vinegar

- Add-Ins:

- 125 g unsweetened shredded coconut

- 90 g chopped dried sweet cherries (optional)

Instructions

1. All ingredients should be at room temperature, 70 – 80 F.
2. Set up the bread pan and beater paddle(s). Add wet ingredients first, followed by dry ingredients into the pan.
3. In a large mixing bowl, combine the dry ingredients.
4. Combine the wet ingredients in a glass measuring cup, then pour into the bread pan. Spread dry ingredients evenly over the wet mixture.
5. Place the bread pan in the machine. Select Quick bread/cake cycle - Loaf size: 1 1/2 pounds/750g - Medium crust. Start the cycle.
6. About 3 minutes into the mixing process, scrape down the sides of the pan and check the dough consistency. Adjust with flour blend or warm water if necessary. After the first kneading cycle, add the coconut and cherries, if using.
7. Let the cycle complete without interruption, including the bake cycle.
8. When baking is done, check the internal temperature (97°C to 99°C). Remove the pan and cool the loaf on a wire rack for a few minutes. Then, invert the pan to remove the loaf and cool it upside down for at least 2 hours before slicing.
9. Store the bread in an airtight container on the counter for up to 3 days. For longer storage, slice, double-wrap tightly, and freeze in a resealable plastic bag for up to 3 months.
10. Note: Ensure the spice blend used is free from potential gluten contamination if seeking a gluten-free option.

CONCLUSION

Finally, this gluten-free bread machine cookbook is more than just a recipe collection; it's a testament to the artistry and joy of baking. It's a recipe that will take you on a flavorful journey, transforming simple ingredients into delectable loaves that will satisfy not only dietary needs but also cravings for exceptional taste and texture.

You've discovered the alchemy of gluten-free baking in these pages, navigating the nuances of alternative flours, binding agents, and flavors. Each recipe invites you to enter a world where creativity and adaptability reign supreme—where the warmth of a freshly baked loaf transcends mere sustenance, becoming a canvas for memories and shared moments with loved ones.

May you have discovered the thrill of experimentation and the joy of discovery as you worked through these recipes. Accept the ups and downs, knowing that each batch represents a step forward, a lesson learned, and a testament to your culinary journey.

This cookbook is more than just about bread; it's a celebration of possibilities, a reminder that dietary restrictions don't have to limit the joys of the table. It's an invitation to enjoy the aroma of success and the satisfaction of making something nutritious and delicious from scratch.

So, as you continue your gluten-free bread machine baking adventure, may these recipes be your companions, guiding you through the twists and turns and providing inspiration and encouragement along the way. May the whirring of the bread machine and the aroma of freshly baked loaves weave stories of joy, perseverance, and the sheer delight of creating something wonderful in your kitchen. Happy baking, and may each slice bring you a smile and warmth in your heart.

Recipe Card Planner

Title

From The Kitchen Of

Yield   Serves

Ingredients

_____

_____

_____

_____

_____

_____

_____

Directions

_____

_____

_____

_____

_____

_____

_____

NOTES

Recipe Card Planner

Title

From The Kitchen Of

Yield   Serves

Ingredients

_____

_____

_____

_____

_____

_____

_____

Directions

_____

_____

_____

_____

_____

_____

_____

NOTES

Recipe Card Planner

Title

From The Kitchen Of

Yield

Serves

Ingredients

_____
_____
_____
_____
_____
_____
_____

Directions

_____
_____
_____
_____
_____
_____
_____

NOTES

Recipe Card Planner

Title

From The Kitchen Of

Yield

Serves

Ingredients

_____

_____

_____

_____

_____

_____

_____

Directions

_____

_____

_____

_____

_____

_____

_____

NOTES

Recipe Card Planner

Title

From The Kitchen Of

Yield   Serves

Ingredients

_____
_____
_____
_____
_____
_____
_____

Directions

_____
_____
_____
_____
_____
_____
_____
_____

NOTES

Recipe Card Planner

Title

From The Kitchen Of

Yield   Serves

Ingredients

Directions

NOTES

Recipe Card Planner

Title _____

From The Kitchen Of _____

Yield _____ Serves _____

Ingredients

_____
_____
_____
_____
_____
_____
_____

Directions

_____
_____
_____
_____
_____
_____
_____
_____

NOTES

Recipe Card Planner

Title

From The Kitchen Of

Yield

Serves

Ingredients

Directions

NOTES

Recipe Card Planner

Title

From The Kitchen Of

Yield   Serves

Ingredients

Directions

NOTES

Recipe Card Planner

Title [   ]

From The Kitchen Of [   ]

Yield [   ]   Serves [   ]

Ingredients

_____
_____
_____
_____
_____
_____
_____

Directions

_____
_____
_____
_____
_____
_____
_____

NOTES

Recipe Card Planner

Title

From The Kitchen Of

Yield   Serves

Ingredients

_____
_____
_____
_____
_____
_____
_____
_____

Directions

_____
_____
_____
_____
_____
_____
_____
_____
_____

NOTES

Recipe Card Planner

Title

From The Kitchen Of

Yield   Serves

Ingredients

_____
_____
_____
_____
_____
_____
_____

Directions

_____
_____
_____
_____
_____
_____
_____
_____

NOTES

Recipe Card Planner

Title

From The Kitchen Of

Yield   Serves

Ingredients

_____
_____
_____
_____
_____
_____
_____
_____
_____
_____

Directions

_____
_____
_____
_____
_____
_____
_____
_____
_____
_____
_____

NOTES

Recipe Card Planner

Title

From The Kitchen Of

Yield

Serves

Ingredients

Directions

NOTES

Recipe Card Planner

Title

From The Kitchen Of

Yield

Serves

Ingredients

Directions

NOTES

Made in United States
Troutdale, OR
11/27/2024

25403931R00049